Meeting Registration
A - L M - Z

Nick Topitzes
with Lori O'Konek

August 2009 Second Printing

Cover Image: J.P. Schmelzer

ISBN 0-9773274-0-X

Acknowledgements

Writing this book has always been a goal. Working with meeting planners each day, my staff and I constantly see little ways to help them. New planners were always taking furious notes in my "Perfecting Your Registration" workshops. So being able to work with Lori O'Konek in getting this done gave me great satisfaction. Lori was able to take my writings, workshops, and checklists and put them into a logical order. I owe her a great deal of thanks. Thanks also to my wonderful staff at pc/nametag that holds down the fort while I am out on the road meeting with planners, running meetings and working with the various associations we participate in. Thanks to my meeting planning friends who helped review the book. Also, thanks to my family who puts up with my absence and my "control freak" moments, especially when I have asked them to help at doing what I love, meeting registration.

Table Of Contents

REGISTRATION MAKES THE MEETING GO 'ROUND

Registration is the nucleus of a successful meeting. Attendees' perceptions of the quality of your event (and the organization presenting it) begins with the very first "Save the Date" postcard. It is enhanced by communication during the advance registration process and is pretty much nailed down when they arrive at on-site registration. Even the most fabulous program will probably not satisfy an attendee who has experienced problems up until this point.

When planning your meeting, visualize the desired experience of the registration process and work backward from there.

> *"First impressions are crucial for success in many fields and meetings are no exception. Whether people are queuing to attend a conference or pre-registering by mail for a seminar, the experience will color their judgment of the event."*
>
> (Professional Meeting Management,
> MPI 1999, page 178)

When it comes to a meeting's success, understand that just about every aspect of the event touches the registration process in some way.

- Registration form and process
- Data collection and use
- Sponsorship generation
- Revenue tracking and collection
- Branding of your meeting, the organization and your partners/sponsors
- Promotion
- Well thought-out supplies and materials that enhance attendees' experience
- Seamless tracking of individuals' choices of seminars, workshops and optional events
- Smooth on-site greeting
- Consistent on-site presence and information
- Evaluation

PERFECTING YOUR REGISTRATION

For the meeting planner, the registration process is an imperative planning and tracking system that can help make or break your success.

With a solid database and registration process, a meeting planner can observe estimates versus actuals to make course corrections along the way. This actually helps you become a better business person and helps in the production of a better meeting.

For the attendee, the registration process must be a seamless series of events that are never even noticed. If it is, it's likely there has been a glitch.

UP FRONT DECISIONS

Before the meeting planner sits down to design the registration process, there are a few decisions that must be made. These are the overarching policies that must be determined, promoted, tracked and executed throughout the entire course. How much will you charge? Will you charge more for registration on-site? What is your cancellation policy? How will you give incentive to those that pay well in advance and, therefore, improve your meeting's cash flow?

These questions need to be answered early in the process so that you can design your registration form, database and materials to clearly outline and promote these policies.

HOW MUCH ARE YOU GOING TO CHARGE?

Especially for a first-time meeting, determining the most appropriate registration cost often causes some consternation. First, you must revisit the goals and objectives you've signed off on with your decision-makers. Your objectives might include driving higher attendance. Or they might direct you to attract a better qualified audience. In any case, your meeting's goals and objectives will guide your pricing decisions.

While some meeting planners are reticent to charge too much for their meeting, it is a proven phenomenon that sometimes raising the cost actually enhances the value of the meeting. Expert meeting planner Anver Suleiman's track record bears this out. He's often the specialist called in to take over meetings in trouble. In his experience, raising the price of the event has actually boosted attendance for many meetings.

DO YOUR HOMEWORK

It's a good idea to do your homework before beginning the discussion about price. Check out what similar meetings charge and the actual turn out of each. Also consider your particular target audience. What are members of this audience accustomed to spending on professional development and networking opportunities such as you're offering?

KEEP IT SIMPLE

Along with determining the overall price of your meeting, you'll need to decide how you will design your pricing strategy. Some meeting planners, in an effort to make the price appear more attractive, offer a relatively low registration price with a variety of extra options. In addition to the basic price, dozens of a la carte items, from individual workshops, to luncheons, to dinners, to various outings, inch up the total registration price. The registrant chooses from the menu and adds up the total cost at the bottom of the order form.

We'd like to warn against this technique. Remember that the actual registration cost for a meeting is only a fraction of what the attendee will have to invest to make the trip. Attendees will either perceive the overall expenditure as a value or they won't. This is a research, programming and marketing issue more than a pricing concern. Potential attendees are not going to be fooled and they certainly won't change their minds over the price-savings of skipping a couple of luncheons.

Also realize, this technique makes it unnecessarily arduous on the staff. With too many choices, it makes data entry and tracking much more complicated and increases the chance for error. We advise to "make it good and keep it simple."

SIGN 'EM UP EARLY
—THE IMPORTANCE OF ADVANCE REGISTRATION

Months ahead of time, when an attendee first signed up for your meeting, it probably seemed like a great idea. However, as the meeting dates approach, many other choices and stresses present themselves, a college buddy is coming home, a huge project came up at the office, a baby daughter is about to take her first steps and the forecasts predict the first spring-like weather in months. Furthermore, the laundry's not done, the bills have to be paid and the concept of a day's worth of planes, trains and taxi cabs is all but pleasant. Now, suddenly, your meeting seems like a really bad idea.

If your attendee hadn't already paid in advance, it'd be a no-brainer to cancel at this late date.

Advance registration is critical to your bottom line. Not only does it dissuade cancellations, it affords the meeting planner cash up front to pay for the many costs incurred before the actual meeting date, such as staffing, marketing and down payments. It's a very risky proposition to finance the entire meeting development phase with the goal of making it all back once the meeting is over.

Advance registration is also critical to effectively manage your meeting. As early registrations come in, you are able to test your assumptions and make course corrections along the way. Perhaps, you'll find that the majority of attendees are not signing up for the gala. You are then able to re-think spending thousands of dollars for that event. Or you might find that everyone wants to attend Workshop A and you'll need to shuffle some things around to allow it a larger room. Even "better than expected" news could be devastating to your meeting if you are caught off guard. What happens if a lot more people show up than you intended? You might need extra staff, extra seating and extra materials. If you're not prepared to accommodate everyone, your meeting will come off as poorly as if no one showed.

By driving people to register early, you will have a much better handle on what to expect. You'll come off looking much more professional and better in charge. And your attendees will realize a better experience.

There's another really important factor in getting the money up front. What about catastrophes? Early registration allows you to lock in your finances. Otherwise, you could spend a whole lot of money planning and promoting your event, but when a major blizzard is predicted, the turnout is dismal. And you're out tens of thousands of dollars.

An effective registration process absolutely should include and promote the opportunity to enroll and pay in advance.

BENEFITS OF ADVANCE REGISTRATION

Advance registration is extremely important to the meeting planner:

- Improves management of cash flow.
- Reduces on-site labor costs.
- Simplifies on-site traffic.
- Helps you plan for food/beverage events and session necessities.
- Controls name badge stock to protect your assets.
- Allows for course correction in program design and marketing as issues or omissions are discovered.

Attendees also enjoy the benefits of pre-registration. Be sure to promote them!

- There will be no need to wait in tedious lines at on-site registration.
- You will receive meeting materials at home, so they can be reviewed on the plane, or will be conveniently waiting for you when you arrive.
- Notice how much money you will save with Early Bird Discounts when you sign up early (if applicable).
- Earn great incentives when you're one of the first to register (if applicable).
- Your space will be guaranteed for events with limited capacity.

A word of caution:

Without a carefully designed plan and adequate procedures, all the benefits of advance registration could be destroyed with a couple lost registrations or misplaced payments. It's critical that a procedure is well-designed and well-trained long before the first attendee registers and follows through to on-site.

Not even the most hyped-up software program will do you any good if the information entered is inconsistent or incorrect or if the procedures are not well understood and observed.

GIVE THEM A REASON TO MAKE YOUR LIFE BETTER

To further accentuate the advantages of advance registration, create and promote a simple, yet enticing strategy to inspire attendees to act in the best interests of your meeting. What's going to make your meeting most successful? You want people to commit and pay early. You probably want to drive attendance up. On the other hand, you might not want more attendees, but rather better qualified ones. You might even want to use your prospect list to do some personal selling for you. Make sure your program and promotion loudly and clearly rewards whichever behaviors you're looking for.

LET YOUR ATTENDEES DO THE SELLING

For example, some meeting planners offer a discount or incentive to organizations who send multiple people. They might offer a lower price when five or more people register. Others reward attendees for making successful referrals.

THE EARLY BIRD GETS THE DEAL

Another approach is to offer different pricing levels according to the date one registers. You might offer a substantial "Early Bird Discount" to those that register very early, maybe two to four months out, depending upon your meeting. Not only is it probably very advantageous to have 75%-90% of the published registration fee in your bank early on to use to produce your meeting, but it also gives you the time to re-sell and lock in the commitment of those attendees.

Next, you might offer the published rate to those that sign up within a week of the conference.

Finally, for those lollygaggers that wait to register on-site or within a week of the conference, you might charge the highest price, one that exceeds the published price. This type of tiered program rewards people for helping you reach your meeting's

ALLCOM CONFERENCE '09

MARCH 1ST, 2009

Conference.........$595

Early Bird Special!
(Must be postmarked by January 15)
................$495

On-Site Registration
................$695

goals. Who in their right mind would part with their money before they absolutely had to, unless, of course, there was a good enough cost benefit? It also helps you avoid the risk and cost of last-minute processing.

REDUCE ON-SITE REGISTRATIONS

On-site registration is expensive. We suggest doing everything you can to minimize the number of attendees who wait until the last minute. Why? Because it's a nuisance. It's expensive. And, it's a very high risk.

You have to handle money, heighten security, deal expediently with credit cards and manage prudent accounting practices under duress.

On-site, accounting procedures often get very sloppy. Everyone's exhausted and everything's moving so fast that it's really difficult to keep everything straight and buttoned up.

Therefore, you have to hire extra staff. Then, they can't be the inexpensive temp employees or volunteers. They have to be trained and possibly bonded. Most likely, you'll want to bring them with you from your staff and if all possible, you'll want to bring along your accountant. One accomplished meeting planner says, "If you register on-site, I really sock it to you."

This type of strategy even works for a free meeting. If you're planning a public meeting that's free of charge, and want to be better prepared and successful, charge those that don't sign up ahead of time. Publicize the fact that those who show up at the door without registering will be charged a nominal fee. This helps you encourage people to sign up so you can plan ahead and be prepared for whomever or how many will show up.

OFFER LOW-COST INCENTIVES TO GET WHAT YOU WANT

As advance registration is so advantageous for the meeting planner, look for creative ways to inspire attendees to take you up on the offer. One meeting planner, for example, offers free entry to the popular Mississippi River Cruise to the first 100 attendees that register for the conference. Other planners offer incentives such as free polo shirts, professional development books and tapes or specialty items such as PDAs, portfolios and briefcases.

Tip:
Some organizations, such as universities, work exclusively with purchase orders. The meeting planner cannot collect these funds until after the event has occurred. You might consider making your early bird discounts or incentives applicable only to those that register and PAY in advance, unless all your attendees must use purchase orders.

CANCELLATIONS/REFUNDS

Every meeting should have a cancellation and refund policy that is visibly publicized and well-integrated into your database design. It's critical to your meeting's reputation that you clearly spell out up front what attendees can expect should they choose to cancel. It's also important that your database and accounting procedure design include the tracking and management of these processes. You'll want to manage information such as: date of cancellation, if refunds are due, when they are due and when they were sent.

Like advance registration policies, you will want to design your cancellation policy to reinforce the behavior you desire without coming off as a tyrant.

It's totally reasonable to charge a nominal fee for all cancellations to cover your processing and back office costs. For example, you might publicize something like "All cancellations are subject to a $25 cancellation fee." Moreover, it's also reasonable to charge a greater fee closer to the event, such as "Any cancellation after February 17 (two to three weeks prior) will be charged a late fee" (perhaps up to 50% of the registration fee). You might even consider not giving out refunds at all for cancellations during the week of the event.

After a well publicized cut-off date, one meeting planner refuses to give back any cash at all. Instead, he'll issue a credit (good for a year) for a portion of the registration fee to be used toward future meetings and/or educational materials from his company. After all, that close to the meeting, he's had to give the hotel, and all other suppliers, a guarantee.

Another consideration is your substitution policy. If ACME company's Betsy Brown isn't able to make the meeting at the last minute, will you allow her office mate, Greta Green to come instead? Have you made provisions in your process to accommodate this type of change? Will you charge a substitution fee for the effort involved with changing the database, materials and badges?

The most important things about designing a cancellation policy is to be forthright and to be firm.

Be loud and clear.

Your intention is not to make money on cancellation fees. You really don't want people to cancel at all. The primary purpose of blatantly publicizing your policy is to discourage people from canceling. The next, of course, is to cover your costs associated with a cancellation. So don't hide it in the fine print. Make your cancellation policy very visible to all.

Walk loudly and carry a small stick.

It's also important to be firm. Set stringent policies to protect yourself and the viability of your meeting. If you are too lenient from the onset, you can't go back and be tougher. On the other hand, if you set strict policy, you can always back off and be more forgiving. You certainly can make an exception for the individual case of an extenuating circumstance such as an illness or death. In fact, it's important to be flexible in these types of situations. The appearance of a lack of sympathy could seriously jeopardize your public image. Set yourself up to be the generous benefactor instead of the mean, stingy ogre.

LIABILITY

To that point, it's critical that you clearly outline the limits to your meeting's liability. Let it be known that you and your organization are not liable for any situations attendees may encounter that are not immediately within the meeting's control. For example, you can't be responsible should the conference be cancelled by a major disaster, such as a flood, a tornado or a 9/11 travesty. You can't be responsible for what every single workshop leader has to say. And you certainly can't be held liable for an attendee's personal travel.

While this may seem obvious and excessive, in this litigious world, the meeting that takes these extra steps will demonstrate to its attendees that it cares about their well-being, while somewhat protecting itself from the rare, but potentially damaging off-the-wall lawsuit. Many meeting planners have seemingly unbelievable stories like this to share: A couple chose to go to a several day, out-of-town business meeting. While they were away at the meeting, the clock radio shorted out and set their house on fire. They returned home to devastation, but then turned around and tried to sue the meeting for their loss. Their claim? It was the meeting's fault because their marketing materials enticed the couple to leave home.

While the claim did not hold up in court and the meeting was not found culpable, it was forced to spend over $20,000 battling the accusations.

Publishing your liability statement certainly doesn't guarantee your protection, but it can help. It helps attendees understand what they are responsible for, helps dissuade some from trying to take advantage and helps the judge see that you have taken

> We do not accept responsibility for personal injury during travel, either to or from the event or anytime on-site, except when attending official functions. We disclaim the validity of all statements, claims, handouts of presenters. Since these are their own representations, they do not necessarily reflect the opinion of management.
>
> Attendees should use prudent judgement. We are not responsible for unsafe or illegal conduct of suppliers, or personnel that are either directly or indirectly involved with the conference. Those who purchase nonrefundable tickets, do so at their own risk. Any photo or video taken of attendees may be used for promotional purposes or resale. Amount of our liability is limited to the amount of registration fees.
>
> © PC/NAMETAG, 2005

all possible precautions.

When writing your liability statement, make it simple and make it clear.

CHOOSE YOUR WEAPONS —USE A MIX OF REGISTRATION VEHICLES

Make it as easy as possible for your attendees to register for your conference. People like to have choices. It makes them feel empowered. Even in this day of "internet everything," there are still many who are more comfortable using the telephone, fax or even, the trusty United States Postal Service, often referred to as "snail mail."

While it might be more convenient to only offer your preferred communication mode, the risks far outweigh the convenience factor. Be sure to make every option possible available for your registrants, even if it means a little more work for you.

Yes, the Web has become a powerful tool for meeting planners. But the truth is, online registration is just another processing channel. When online registration was first introduced, it was touted as the answer to all the meeting planner's problems. It would reduce cost and eliminate errors.

If you aren't careful, using the web for registration can cost as much or more than the traditional channels of direct mail, fax and phone. Moreover, it doesn't necessarily reduce errors. Even if the erroneous data entry is not your staff's fault, it will still pose problems for you.

You know the saying, "Garbage in. Garbage out." If an attendee enters faulty information, it will filter through the process and become the meeting planner's issue. When the registrant shows up at your registration table to receive a badge with a misspelled name—even if he or she was the one to type it in—it remains the meeting planner's responsibility to produce a correction.

However, don't shy away from the Web either. It can be an efficient and effective vehicle. It's expected with the younger generation. In addition, it is a relatively safe method of transaction.

With encryption technology, one probably incurs more risk by leaving a credit card receipt in the garbage than by paying for something on a secured online site. Those that are smart enough to hack into an encrypted site to steal a credit card number are probably otherwise occupied making a heck of a lot more money doing something else.

The most effective registration process is a combination of traditional and newer channels. So, make each available and make certain that your systems are set up to accommodate each. Know your audience and make it as easy as possible for anyone to sign up.

DESIGNING YOUR REGISTRATION FORM & DATABASE

No two meetings are alike. Each meeting's registration process is likely to be unique. The process needed for a one-day seminar will likely be very simple, whereas a several day meeting, with hotel accommodations and an optional golf outing, will be much more complex.

For example, if you're planning a conference for an association, booking the hotel rooms may be the individuals' responsibility. On the other hand, if you are handling hotel arrangements, you'll have to carefully plan your database to accommodate which hotel all attendees choose, what type of room they're requesting and even with whom they are sharing.

Registration forms and the resulting database screens need to be customized to fit the specific needs of each individual meeting.

A well-thought out process will become your best ally and most important meeting management tool. As the registration process is so critical to the success of your entire meeting, it is important that you pay a lot of attention to its design from the very beginning.

THE CHICKEN OR THE EGG?

Now, just where do you start? The form or the database? Well, both, kind of. You're likely to find this to be an interactive process with a couple of passes needed before you're completely satisfied with what you have. The challenge is that now you have to anticipate and account for any possible issues that will arise much later in the process.

Usually, the most logical approach is to begin with the registration form. When you're comfortable with it, start the design of the database and entry windows. If you're able to do this early enough, you'll be able to integrate any omissions or challenges you discover into the registration form before it has to go to print.

There are three words you'll want to remember when designing your database. Simple. Consistent. Standardized.

consistent simple standardized

First, you want to make using your database as simple as possible. You might want to consider using a unique identification number for each individual entry, which you can also use as a confirmation number. This technique makes it a lot easier to tell if two Jane Johnsons from NYC have signed up for your conference or if you have duplicate entries.

Also be sure to use unique fields for each piece of information. The more unique fields you have, the better you can manipulate the data. At this early phase of the process, you can't be certain which information you will need later on, so you'll want to make sure it's as flexible as possible. For example, instead of using a field called "Full Name," separate them into two fields called "First Name" and "Last Name" so you can sort by the last name. It's simpler to do this from the beginning than having to go back and separate this information later. Finally, leave some spaces for unexpected information. Say three months into the process, the CEO wants to have a golf outing. Now you have a space to add this information.

Next, design your database and input screens to be consistent with your registration form. When the input screens follow the same order as the registration form, it makes it a lot quicker for data entry. It also reduces errors as you are a lot less likely to miss entering data if it follows sequentially.

Finally, create your database entry process to result in standardized information and spelling. Pull-down menus are an excellent way to achieve this. By using pull-down menus for various options offered to attendees, you will speed up the entry process and eliminate the potential of ending up with a variety of ways to describe a single choice. If information is not standardized, when you go to sort the information, it won't sort properly, and you could easily miss some of the information.

For example, if you allow data entry personnel to key in the workshop choices, one person might key in "*Session #1—Marketing With the Big Fish*" and another might enter "*Marketing Big Fish.*" The sort feature will not cluster the two variations together and you'll have to do a lot of hand work to capture the true totals of each workshop session.

On the other hand, if there's a pull-down menu with all of the workshop options listed, there's no chance of everything not being standardized. Pull-down menus are appropriate for any choices you're offering: hotel selection, hotel room preferences, workshop sessions and optional events. You could also use them for membership status, salutations, suffixes or areas of residence. The extra up front effort will greatly reduce the amount of work needed later.

DESIGNING YOUR REGISTRATION FORM

It is through the registration form that you will collect all the various pieces of information you'll need. These tools will dictate the design of your database. And it's this information that will allow you to generate the types of reports you will need to track meeting statistics before the meeting and after the meeting for planning next year's event.

First, you will need to sit down and figure out what information you need to produce a really good meeting. What information will you need for nametags, reports, financial tracking and post-meeting evaluation?

Start by reviewing last year's registration form. Was there anything you wished you would have included that you didn't? Is there anything you can do this year to make the data entry and processing easier? Are you adding anything this year that you'll have to account for? Next check out other meetings' registration forms. It's a good idea to keep a file of all those registration forms you get in the mail to use as research for designing your next one. You'll be able to pick up tips and tricks from others. You might see something that you hadn't thought of before.

When working with optional events and outside coordinators, work with them to make sure you've included the collection of all the information they'll need.

WHAT'YA WANT TO KNOW?

Clearly, you'll need to know who's registering for your meeting. Your registration form will have to capture any personal information you might need from this moment on through the post-meeting follow up. Of course, you will need to include the obvious; name, address, phone, title and organization.

Attendee information

In addition, you'll want to make sure that you have all possible ways to contact a registrant in the case of needing more information, sending out confirmations or alerting attendees of late-breaking news. Be sure to ask for a day-time phone, a night-time phone, a cell phone and a fax number. Also request e-mail addresses as this is often the most expedient way to get important news to the majority of your attendees.

ATTENDEE INFO

- ❑ First Name
- ❑ Middle Initial
- ❑ Last name
- ❑ Address
- ❑ City
- ❑ State
- ❑ Zip
- ❑ Day Phone
- ❑ Night Phone
- ❑ Cell Phone
- ❑ Fax
- ❑ E-mail Address

Badge name

Nametags are probably the single most important factor in your meeting's success. They're a great icebreaker and a fundamental networking tool. So you will need to capture the exact information the attendee will want displayed when it finally comes to designing your badges. In the U.S., it is most common to print a person's first name or nickname in large bold font on the badge. This technique promotes networking because it makes it easy to read another's first name from far away. If an attendee can't recall another's name, this is a helpful memory jogger. Experts suggest that this name should be large enough to read from up to ten feet away.

So, it's important to specifically request the name one would like to have on their badge. For example, if you don't ask for a badge name, Mr. Xaiver Summers, whom everyone knows as Frank, might be a little reticent to wear a badge that invites everyone to call him by his formal name. On the other hand, if you don't ask for the formal business name, someone might receive the coveted Board of Director's award with "Bucky" engraved on it.

This custom, however, is unique to the United States. In European countries, for example, name badges are smaller and more formal. Don't make the mistake of using the large nickname technique if you're planning a meeting for an overseas organization.

Also be aware that doctors and clergy don't tend to like the "first name only" style. In these cases, it's best to play it safe and use the more formal approach.

SALUTATION

- ❑ Mr.
- ❑ Ms.
- ❑ Mrs.
- ❑ Dr.
- ❑ Prof.
- ❑ Fr.
- ❑ Rev.
- ❑ Bishop

Salutation

Next, you will need to consider whether you'll want to know your attendees' preferred salutations. For some formal meetings and in many European countries, nametags will need to include "Fr., Mr., Ms., Dr., or Prof."

Even if you don't plan on using a formal salutation on the badge, you might want to have them in your database for confirmation letters, next year's marketing campaign or future recognition.

Suffixes

You should also request suffix information in the case that you might need it. You will want to include, "Jr., Sr., or III" for formal use and mailings. In addition, for certain meetings, you might want to include certain designations, such as CMP, M.D., D.D., or Ph.D. Conversely, if you are holding a meeting for medical doctors, it might seem redundant to include the suffix as everyone attending will be an M.D.

SUFFIXES

- ❑ B.A. (Bachelor of Arts)
- ❑ M.A. (Master of Arts)
- ❑ M.D. (Medical Doctor)
- ❑ L.L.D. (Doctor of Law)
- ❑ D.D. (Doctor of Divinity)
- ❑ D.D.S. (Doctor of Dental Surgery)
- ❑ B.S. (Bachelor of Science)
- ❑ M.B.A. (Masters of Business Administration)
- ❑ Ph.D. (Doctor of Philosophy)
- ❑ Ed.D. (Doctor of Education)
- ❑ J.D. (Doctor of Jurisprudence)
- ❑ M.Ed. (Master of Education)
- ❑ Jr. (Junior)
- ❑ Sr. (Senior)
- ❑ III (The Third)

Company & title

There are times when showcasing an attendee's company and title on a name badge is critical, while there are other times when it's not. At a trade show, your exhibitors will appreciate knowing to whom they are talking. They will want to know who's a potential customer and who's not. However, at the National Sales Convention for The Big Beer Brewery, it's not important to include the company name because everyone there will be representing it.

Another consideration is whether to make either the company name or the title larger on the badge. Is it more important, for example, at the annual restaurant trade show to highlight that an attendee works for Big Hamburger Mogul or whether he or she is a national buyer versus counter help.

Residence

For many national or international meetings, it's important to display where each attendee resides. It's nice to know whether the person you're sharing lunch with is from England or South Carolina. It can also provide fodder for ice breaking conversations, "Hey, I used to live in Milwaukee. Is that famous fifty's style custard place still there?" For your convenience, you'll find a list of abbreviations in the Registration Tool Box. You might consider adding these to a drop down menu in your database for easy and accurate input.

Membership status

Another piece of information you're likely to want on hand is the membership status of each attendee. This information will be needed if you offer discounts to attendees of a certain status or if you want to honor various members with ribbons on their name badges. This is an excellent and inexpensive way to give recognition to those that have been volunteering their time and talents all year long or to those who continue their membership with your organization.

MEMBERSHIP STATUS

- ❑ Member
- ❑ Foundation
- ❑ Past President
- ❑ Director
- ❑ New or First Timer
- ❑ Donor
- ❑ Union
- ❑ Associated
- ❑ Full
- ❑ Honorary
- ❑ Retired
- ❑ Supporting

Method of payment and payment status

Your accountant will likely be most interested in the area of your registration form dedicated to attendees' payments. Make it easy on yourself and your staff by keeping this section as simple and clear as possible. Use check boxes, if possible, to clearly delineate which payment options you offer. Then, when you go to design your datbase, consider using the same choices as dropdown menus to make data entry easier. You'll want to designate how your registrant chooses to pay; check, credit card or cash, purchase order or state voucher. Often times, government agencies and educational institutions work only with purchase orders or vouchers. It's important to capture all pertinent information so that you can follow up with the appropriate invoices and statements.

METHOD OF PAYMENT

- ❑ Cash
- ❑ Purchase order
- ❑ Credit card
- ❑ State voucher
- ❑ Card number
- ❑ Expiration number
- ❑ Check
- ❑ Drawn on US Bank
- ❑ International $$
- ❑ Date of registration
- ❑ Date of cancellation
- ❑ Refund sent
- ❑ Refund due
- ❑ Cancellation fee
- ❑ Complimentary
- ❑ Member discount
- ❑ Credit Card
  - ❑ MasterCard
  - ❑ Visa
  - ❑ Discover
  - ❑ American Express
  - ❑ Diner's Club

If you will be hosting an international audience, you will have to design your registration form and process to accommodate foreign monies. If you accept other currencies, your bank will charge you a percentage to exchange them. You can avoid this situation by either stating on your registration "Payable in US funds" or by opening a Euro account. In any case, you will need to include check boxes and spaces to prompt the registrant to give you all the proper information you'll need.

You'll also want to include options for complimentary admissions and all possible discounts.

Cancellation policy

Make sure that you include your cancellation policy in your registration form.

Arrival information

Next, you may need to acquire arrival information, especially if you are providing transportation to some or all of your guests. Some meeting planners also want to capture this type of information for security measures. And you'll certainly want to know this to better accommodate your customers, special guests, VIPs and speakers. Design your database in the same order with the same information.

ARRIVAL INFORMATION

- ❑ Arrival date
- ❑ Arrival time
- ❑ Arrival flight
- ❑ Arrival airline
- ❑ Pick-up
- ❑ Taxi
- ❑ Limo
- ❑ Car rental
- ❑ Departure date
- ❑ Departure time
- ❑ Departure flight
- ❑ Departure airline

Rooming Information

List hotel room options so there can be no confusion. Again, if possible, design your registration form with multiple choice check boxes and your database with corresponding drop-down menus of all possible hotel room options.

ROOMING INFORMATION

- ❑ Smoking or non-smoking
- ❑ Late arrival
- ❑ Suite
- ❑ Concierge level
- ❑ Single, double, triple or quad
- ❑ Rate choices
- ❑ Roll-away
- ❑ Studio Suite
- ❑ 1 BR Suite
- ❑ 2 BR Suite
- ❑ VIP Suite
- ❑ Sharing with
  - ❑ ________________

Do they want a smoking or a non-smoking room? Do they want a double bed or two singles? Do they want to spend the extra money to be on the concierge level? If they will be sharing a room, with whom will they be sharing? It's important to design a feature in your database that cross references this information for both attendees. If Bob Johnson signs up to share a room with Bill Kennedy, but Bill signs up with Dale Skies, you will want to clear that up before they arrive at the property.

Hotel selection

In addition, you'll want to include choices for the various properties that you are making available to your attendees. Again offer multiple choice check boxes instead of allowing attendees to write in the hotel names. You'd be surprised how much this simple effort can reduce your stress.

Take, for example, a city like Washington D.C., where there are multiple properties owned by the same company. If your registrant just writes in "Hyatt," how will you know which one was intended? The Grand Hyatt Washington? The Park Hyatt Washington? Or Hyatt Regency Washington on Capitol Hill? Now, you'll have to track down the registrant to find out or risk picking the wrong option. Give attendees an easy-to-use series of check boxes so they are very clear about the choices they are requesting.

Likewise, the same type of forward thinking can avoid confusion when it comes to data entry. Instead of asking staff to type in the name of the hotel, offer them a corresponding drop-down menu that lists the same options as you've identified on your registration form. If you don't do this and have several different people entering information, you could end up what looks like a dozen different hotels. One person enters "Hyatt on the Hill," another enters "Hyatt Regency" and still another enters "Hyatt Washington." When you go to sort the information to determine how many shuttle buses you will need to send, you won't know which are which or how many you'll need.

HOTEL

❑ Best Western
❑ Comfort Inn
❑ Courtyard
❑ Crowne Plaza
❑ Days Inn
❑ Doubletree
❑ Embassy Suites Hotel
❑ Fairmont
❑ Four Seasons
❑ Grand Hyatt
❑ Hampton Inn
❑ Hilton
❑ Holiday Inn
❑ Howard Johnson
❑ Hyatt on the Hill
❑ Inter-Continental
❑ Marriott
❑ Meridien
❑ Omni Hotel
❑ Radisson
❑ Ramada
❑ Renaissance
❑ Residence Inn
❑ Ritz-Carlton
❑ Sheraton
❑ Westin Hotels & Resorts
❑ Wyndham

VIP treatment

Another area you will want to consider when designing your database is the management of hotel suites and special treatment. Will you need any hospitality suites? Who will be assigned to those rooms? Do you need to arrange for special suites for VIPs? You'll want to keep close track or you could end up with mud on your face when the President of the Board finds out she only got a studio suite while your meeting planner accidentally ended up in the Presidential Suite.

Consult the hotel information list when creating your registration form and database.

Workshop sign up

There are several ways to handle workshop sign up. Some meeting planners choose to publicize the date and time of all workshops to allow the registrant to determine their schedule during the early registration process.

There are pros and cons to this method. On the pro side, with these decisions made up front, there is no on-site processing. In addition, if you know how many people are planning to attend each session, you can do a better job of planning. You can juggle the location of each session contingent upon how many people signed up. You can plan for special AV needs if a workshop needs to go into overflow accommodations.

On the con side, if you publicize the dates and times of all your sessions in the marketing brochure, you're pretty locked in. A potential attendee might see three different workshops he or she's interested in, but if they're all offered at the same time, it might be the deal breaker when deciding whether to attend your meeting. Also, you don't have the ability to move around workshops once they're publicized. If you simply list the workshop offerings, you can sometimes schedule them according to the response in your Early Bird Registration.

Some other things you might take into consideration when setting up your database are size limits for each session and CEU tracking. For your own convenience, you might consider assigning a numeric code to each of your workshop sessions. One meeting planner for example, assigns 100 numbers for all those workshops offered in the first period, 200s for the second period and so on.

Optional events

If you are offering optional events, you will have to make room for these in your registration form and database. Whether or not you are charging extra money for each option, you will want to be able to track how many are planning to attend. If you are charging for each event, you will want to make sure that your database is compatible with your accounting department's systems.

Optional events can include food/beverage events such as luncheons, dinners, networking breakfasts or special banquets. Other possibilities include additional activities like field trips to local attractions, such as to Universal Studios in Orlando, a trip to the Grand Canyon in Vegas or a tour of the bayou country in New Orleans. Other planners offer special events they've designed and organized. For these, accurate numbers are even more important. Options might include pre-conference seminars, aerobic classes, fun runs, tennis tournaments or golf outings. For a golf outing, don't forget to ask for a golfer's handicap, what kind of cart they want and their preferred foursome, if relevant. Be certain to plan ahead and capture all the information you will need to make your event a success.

Diet

The successful meeting planner will do everything possible to make each attendee comfortable. One area where a meeting planner can really come out a hero is with attendees' special dietary concerns. If you ask the right questions up front, you can painlessly make special accommodations that not only make the experience more pleasant, but will also save you and the hotel staff headaches during the meeting.

It's important to invite registrants to tell you about their special dietary requirements ahead of the meeting. In addition, you will want to clarify the attendees' requests. Whether the request is a meal plan that's Kosher, Diabetic or Vegetarian, Low-salt or Low-carb, it's in your best interest to get more and better information about your attendees' wishes. After all, your guests probably won't be satisfied with house salads all week long.

For example, there's a wide variety of definitions for the word vegetarian…

WHAT TYPE OF VEGETARIAN ARE YOU?

SEMI-VEGETARIAN
Dairy foods, eggs, chicken & fish but no other animal flesh

PESCO-VEGETARIAN
Dairy foods, eggs & fish but no animal flesh

LACTO-OVA-VEGETARIAN
Dairy foods & eggs but no animal flesh

OVA-VEGETARIAN
Eggs but no dairy foods or animal flesh

VEGAN
No animal foods of any type

The more information you can give to a chef ahead of time, the better. Your guests will be impressed that you haven't done "the least you can do."

Tip:
Have you ever noticed that in most convention and banquet settings, all special meals are served later than the standard meals? No, this is not a display of discrimination, it's a way to manage customer expectations.

Imagine this. The meeting planner orders ten vegetarian meals. The wait staff starts delivering the fifth chicken meal of the week, and fresh opulent fruit salads for the vegetarians. Suddenly, half the room "remembers" that they, too, are vegetarians and now want to make a special request. Typically, regular meals are provided first so no "sudden vegetarians" appear just as dinner is served.

One way to get around this is to hand out special meal tickets for all those that request them ahead of time. Attendees who have made special dietary arrangements simply hand the wait staff the proper ticket. Be certain, however, to make sure everyone knows this ahead of time. This is a good subject to add to your list of "housekeeping topics" announcements at the opening of the meeting. This type of system usually solves the problem for everyone.

Foreign meetings

If you are planning a meeting out of the country, you will need to plan ahead for acquiring information specific to overseas travel. You'll want information such as each individual's passport number, a list of their vaccines, their insurance and their emergency contact information.

Hint:
It's also a good idea to get photocopies of each attendee's passport. If one of your guests accidentally misplaces his or her passport, you'll be there to save the day instead of being in the midst of a huge hassle while in a foreign system.

Other valuable information

With today's technology, a meeting planner can capture, track and employ a vast array of useful information. You might want to query your registrants about their buying habits or per year purchase amounts. On an aggregate level, this can be very useful for attracting next year's exhibitors. You might track SIC codes to better plan for this and future meetings. In addition, new bar coding technology can gather and hold a lot of information. If you plan to use this technology, you'll want to build a database that will handle it.

Americans with Disabilities Act

It's very important for meeting planners to understand and comply with the Americans with Disabilities Act (ADA).

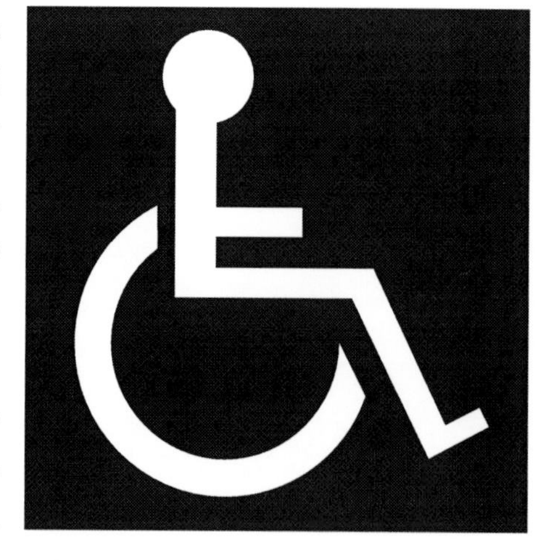

This is a civil rights statute that promises equal access to opportunities in education, employment and society for people with disabilities. The general rule states that: "No individual shall be discriminated against on the basis of disability in the full and equal enjoyment of the goods, services, facilities, privileges, advantages, or accommodations by any person who owns, leases (or leases to), or operates a place of public accommodation."

By law, a person with a disability is anyone with physical or mental impairment that substantially limits one or more activities of daily life. This includes people who are blind, visually impaired, deaf, hearing impaired, mobility impaired, or with psychological disabilities, chronic health impairments, learning disabilities or cognitive limitations.

According to the law, both the facility and the sponsoring organization are equally responsible for providing reasonable accommodations. For you as a meeting manager, you will want to book facilities that are ADA compliant and that you factor in ways to make reasonable accommodation for disabled participants.

The law requires "reasonable accommodation" that does not pose a direct threat to the health or safety of others, doesn't require substantial alteration in the way business is conducted or doesn't present an undue financial or administrative hardship to the business. The intent of the law is to allow full participation of a great number of potential attendees who may have been underrepresented in the past. It is not intended to present a great hardship or hurdles for the meeting planner or the facilities.

The key to staying in compliance is communication. You must make it possible for persons with disabilities to identify themselves early enough for you to be able to accommodate them.

Therefore, your registration form should boldly display the ADA symbol which alerts potential attendees that you're willing to work with them and to communicate to you what they need.

It's important to dedicate a section of your registration form to allow individuals to describe their needs. It is advisable to personally follow up with these individuals to clarify their needs and make sure that you are doing all you can to help them fully participate. It's also important to design your database so that you can document the outcome of your communication and follow through to ensure the requests are provided.

It's not possible to stress enough the importance of this early communication. First, it makes it possible for you to adequately prepare for the accommodations. When you put the ADA symbol in your brochure you are letting people know that you'd like them to notify you in advance. That gives you the capability to do something about the situation. You are giving yourself reasonable time. It is very difficult to try to accommodate special circumstances on a turn of a dime.

For example, if a hearing-impaired individual registers for your meeting and requests an interpreter, you must provide one by law. If you know about this ahead of time, you can make arrangements. Depending upon the duration of your sessions, you'll likely need to hire two or more interpreters for each concurrent session because it is physically challenging for anyone to sign for long stretches at a time. A single person can only sign for up to one-half hour at a time, less if there are multiple or fast-talking speakers.

Second, having displayed the ADA symbol on your registration form and clearly inviting individuals to make you aware of their needs in advance, you've protected yourself. Should a disabled individual show up on site without having informed you, it is not *reasonable* to expect that you can fully provide for their needs.

You might not even be able to find an interpreter with only a couple hours notice. If you are, you're likely to be charged more for the short turn-around. Should you find yourself in court in such a situation, the fact that you gave attendees the chance to allow you to accommodate them with advance notice, could be all the judge would need to rule in your favor.

There are many things you can do to make a disabled attendee's meeting experience more satisfying. For visual-impaired individuals, you might have someone there to read them the notes or provide water bowls for guide dogs. For those in wheel chairs, you might notch out areas of seating to accommodate them. After all, just because one is in a wheel chair, doesn't mean they always want to be relegated to the back or side of the room. And for those with learning disabilities or ADD, you might make special arrangements if testing will be required.

Each person with a disability is an individual. Each is the best expert of what exactly would be most helpful to him or her. Be sure to communicate and don't be afraid to ask what they need.

There are many resources available to help you become more familiar with ADA and ways you can make your meeting more enriching and accessible. You are likely to find your own life enhanced by the experience of helping someone who otherwise might not be able to fully enjoy all the benefits you have to offer.

Emergency contact information

The well-prepared meeting planner also collects emergency contact information, just in case. However, it's important to make sure that this information is tracked and available at anytime during the meeting.

DESIGNING YOUR DATABASE

Now that you know all the information you need to know, which software will you use to store it?

That answer depends upon how robust you want your database and analysis to be.

There are a variety of off-the-shelf software packages available ranging in price from $250 to $10,000 for a fully integrated meeting planning system that ties into accounting and other departments. Software designed simply to create nametags can cost as little as $50.

There are basic software packages that can be adapted to suit your meetings needs. These include: D-base, Excel and Access. However, to get these packages to do what you want them to do, you'll have to either be very proficient in setting them up or you will have to hire a consultant to set it up for you.

There are also off-the-shelf products especially designed for the type of database management a meeting planner needs. These brands include: pc/nametag® PRO X™, Phoenix Solutions MEI, Peopleware, Inc. (CEUs) Conference Planner and ACEware.

Remember, when designing your database:

- Keep it simple, consistent and standardized.
- Use drop-down menus whenever possible.
- Allow room for changes and additions down the road.
- If you're dealing with international audiences, make certain that your database design will accommodate foreign conventions, such as the tilde (ñ), umlaut (ü) and cedilla (ç).

If you're interested in more information about perfecting your registration process, check out these resources:

The Complete Idiot's Guide to Meeting and Event Planning by Alpha Books.

Professional Meeting Management—A European Handbook by Meeting Professionals International.

Professional Meeting Management by Professional Convention Management Association Education Foundation.

ATTENDEE REGISTRATION CHECKLIST

PERSONAL INFORMATION
- ❑ Salutation
- ❑ First name
- ❑ Middle initial
- ❑ Last name
- ❑ Badge name
- ❑ Title
- ❑ Organization
- ❑ Address
- ❑ Suite
- ❑ City
- ❑ State
- ❑ Zip code
- ❑ Postal code
- ❑ Country
- ❑ Phone
- ❑ Fax
- ❑ E-mail address

SALUTATION
- ❑ Mr.
- ❑ Ms.
- ❑ Mrs.
- ❑ Dr.
- ❑ Prof.
- ❑ Fr.

SUFFIX
- ❑ B.A. (Bachelor of Arts)
- ❑ M.A. (Master of Arts)
- ❑ M.D. (Medical Doctor)
- ❑ L.L.D. (Doctor of Law)
- ❑ D.D. (Doctor of Divinity)
- ❑ D.D.S. (Doctor of Dental Surgery)
- ❑ B.S. (Bachelor of Science)
- ❑ M.B.A. (Masters of Business Administration)
- ❑ Ph.D. (Doctor of Philosophy)
- ❑ Ed.D. (Doctor of Education)
- ❑ J.D. (Doctor of Jurisprudence)
- ❑ M.Ed. (Master of Education)
- ❑ Jr.
- ❑ Sr.
- ❑ III

MEMBERSHIP STATUS
- ❑ Member
- ❑ Foundation
- ❑ Past president
- ❑ Director
- ❑ New or first timer
- ❑ Donor
- ❑ Union
- ❑ Associated
- ❑ Full
- ❑ Honorary
- ❑ Retired
- ❑ Supporting

METHOD OF PAYMENT
- ❑ Cash
- ❑ Purchase order
- ❑ State voucher
- ❑ Check
- ❑ Drawn on US bank
- ❑ International $$
- ❑ Date of registration
- ❑ Date of cancellation
- ❑ Refund sent
- ❑ Refund due
- ❑ Cancellation fee
- ❑ Complimentary
- ❑ Member discount
- ❑ Credit card
  - ❑ MasterCard
  - ❑ Visa
  - ❑ Discover
  - ❑ American Express
  - ❑ Diner's Club

ARRIVAL INFORMATION
- ❑ Arrival date
- ❑ Arrival time
- ❑ Arrival flight
- ❑ Arrival airline
- ❑ Pick-up
- ❑ Taxi
- ❑ Limo
- ❑ Car rental
- ❑ Departure date
- ❑ Departure time
- ❑ Departure flight
- ❑ Departure airline

ROOMING INFORMATION
- ❑ Smoking or non-smoking
- ❑ Late arrival
- ❑ Suite
- ❑ Concierge level
- ❑ Single, double, triple or quad
- ❑ Rate choices
- ❑ Roll-away
- ❑ Suite
- ❑ Studio suite
- ❑ 1 BR suite
- ❑ 2 BR suite
- ❑ VIP suite
- ❑ Sharing with
  - ❑ ____________

HOTEL
- ❑ Best Western
- ❑ Comfort Inn
- ❑ Courtyard
- ❑ Crowne Plaza
- ❑ Days Inn
- ❑ Doubletree
- ❑ Embassy Suites Hotel
- ❑ Fairmont
- ❑ Four Seasons
- ❑ Hampton Inn
- ❑ Hilton
- ❑ Holiday Inn
- ❑ Howard Johnson
- ❑ Hyatt
- ❑ Inter-Continental
- ❑ Marriott
- ❑ Meridien
- ❑ Omni Hotel
- ❑ Radisson
- ❑ Ramada
- ❑ Renaissance
- ❑ Residence Inn
- ❑ Ritz-Carlton
- ❑ Sheraton
- ❑ Westin Hotels & Resorts
- ❑ Wyndham

OTHER INFO
- ❑ Speaker
- ❑ Friend
- ❑ Workshop choices
- ❑ Numeric coding
- ❑ Titles
- ❑ CEUs
- ❑ Size limits

OPTIONAL PROGRAMS
- ❑ Golf
- ❑ Tennis
- ❑ Pre-tour
- ❑ Post-tour
- ❑ Banquet
- ❑ Reception
- ❑ Cruise
- ❑ Aerobics

OTHER
- ❑ Golf
- ❑ Handicap
- ❑ Cart
- ❑ Arrival time
- ❑ Foursome
- ❑ Fees due
- ❑ Fees paid

FEES
- ❑ Fees due
- ❑ Date of registration
- ❑ Date of payment
- ❑ Amount paid
- ❑ Method of payment

DISABILITY INFORMATION
- ❑ Hearing impaired (Require arrival time)
- ❑ Wheelchair
- ❑ Visually impaired (Require arrival time)
- ❑ Require disabled room
- ❑ Crutches
- ❑ Foreign Language
- ❑ Attention Deficit Disorder

DIET
- ❑ Kosher
- ❑ Diabetic
- ❑ Low salt
- ❑ No salt
- ❑ Low carb
- ❑ Semi-vegetarian—dairy foods, eggs, chicken & fish but no other animal flesh
- ❑ Pesco-vegetarian—dairy foods, eggs & fish but no animal flesh
- ❑ Lacto-ova-vegetarian—dairy foods & eggs but no animal flesh
- ❑ Ova-vegetarian—eggs but no dairy foods or animal flesh
- ❑ Vegan—no animal foods of any type

FOREIGN
- ❑ Passport #
- ❑ Vaccine
- ❑ Insurance

EMERGENCY CONTACT
- ❑ Name
- ❑ Day phone
- ❑ Night phone
- ❑ Cell phone
- ❑ Relationship

RESIDENCE CHECKLIST

UNITED STATES ABBREVIATIONS

- ❑ AL (Alabama)
- ❑ AK (Alaska)
- ❑ AS (American Samoa)
- ❑ AZ (Arizona)
- ❑ AR (Arkansas)
- ❑ CA (California)
- ❑ CO (Colorado)
- ❑ CT (Connecticut)
- ❑ DE (Delaware)
- ❑ DC (District of Columbia)
- ❑ FM (Federated States of Micronesia)
- ❑ FL (Florida)
- ❑ GA (Georgia)
- ❑ GU (Guam)
- ❑ HI (Hawaii)
- ❑ ID (Idaho)
- ❑ IL (Illinois)
- ❑ IN (Indiana)
- ❑ IA (Iowa)
- ❑ KS (Kansas)
- ❑ KY (Kentucky)
- ❑ LA (Louisiana)
- ❑ ME (Maine)
- ❑ MH (Marshall Islands)
- ❑ MD (Maryland)
- ❑ MA (Massachusetts)
- ❑ MI (Michigan)
- ❑ MN (Minnesota)
- ❑ MS (Mississippi)
- ❑ MO (Missouri)
- ❑ MT (Montana)
- ❑ NE (Nebraska)
- ❑ NV (Nevada)
- ❑ NH (New Hampshire)
- ❑ NJ (New Jersey)
- ❑ NM (New Mexico)
- ❑ NY (New York)
- ❑ NC (North Carolina)
- ❑ ND (North Dakota)
- ❑ MP (Northern Mariana Islands)
- ❑ OH (Ohio)
- ❑ OK (Oklahoma)
- ❑ OR (Oregon)
- ❑ PW (Palau)
- ❑ PA (Pennsylvania)
- ❑ PR (Puerto Rico)
- ❑ RI (Rhode Island)
- ❑ SC (South Carolina)
- ❑ SD (South Dakota)
- ❑ TN (Tennessee)
- ❑ TX (Texas)
- ❑ UT (Utah)
- ❑ VT (Vermont)
- ❑ VI (Virgin Islands)
- ❑ VA (Virginia)
- ❑ WA (Washington)
- ❑ WV (West Virginia)
- ❑ WI (Wisconsin)
- ❑ WY (Wyoming)

CANADIAN PROVINCE ABBREVIATIONS

- ❑ BC (British Columbia)
- ❑ AB (Alberta)
- ❑ SK (Saskatchewan)
- ❑ MB (Manitoba)
- ❑ ON (Ontario)
- ❑ NB (New Brunswick)
- ❑ NF (Newfoundland)
- ❑ NS (Nova Scotia)
- ❑ PE (Prince Edward Island)
- ❑ PQ (Quebec)
- ❑ YT (Yukon Territory)

SAMPLE REGISTRATION FORM #1

REGISTRATION FORM

Please enter your personalized customer code from the address panel: ____________________

Please enroll me in the following seminars:

Seminar Name	Date	Course Code

Name: ____________________

Company: ____________________

Address: ____________________

____

Day Phone: __________ **Home Phone:** __________

Email: ____________________

PAYMENT

❑ Enclosed is my check or money order, made payable to **IRIS COUNTY COMMUNITY COLLEGE**

❑ Please charge to the following credit card: ❑ VISA ❑ MasterCard ❑ Discover ❑ American Express

Card Number: __________ **Expiration Date:** __________

Cardholders name as printed on credit card: ____________________

Signature: ____________________

MAIL to Iris County Community College—Registration Center • Department 1717 • 4877 W. Hickory Trail • Monroe, IN 38507-7897

CALL Iris County Community College at (888) 333-4444 (TDD 888-222-8888)

FAX Iris County Community College at (888) 333-5555 (must include payments by credit card or purchase order.)

VOLUNTARY INFORMATION (This information will be used for planning and program improvements.)

❑ Female ❑ Male Birthdate: Month ______ Day______ Year ________

❑ African American ❑ American Indian/Alaskan Native ❑ Asian/Pacific Islander ❑ Hispanic/Latino ❑ White ❑ Other__________

Are you enrolled in this program primarily for career purposes? ❑ Yes ❑ No

OCCUPATION: ❑ Agriculture/Forestry ❑ Manufacturing ❑ Education ❑ Engineering ❑ Financial Services ❑ Health Services ❑ Protective Services ❑ Government ❑ Retail ❑ Marketing/Advertising ❑ Transportation ❑ Social Services ❑ Communication ❑ Other____________________

If you require special accommodations, please advise us at least two weeks in advance of the event. All requests are kept strictly confidential. We are happy to serve you.

SAMPLE REGISTRATION FORM #2

HOW TO REGISTER

REGISTRATION WILL CLOSE ON MARCH 1, 2009. AFTER MARCH 1, 2009, YOU MAY REGISTER ON SITE AT THE CONFERENCE.

Your registration includes 5 workshops of your choice, seminar materials, lunch and refreshments during breaks. Registration will be confirmed within one week prior to the date of the seminar. For further information, please feel free to call 1-800-333-4444.

Payment:
Your completed registration form must be accompanied by full payment in order to be processed. Please choose the method of payment that is most convenient to you.

Cancellations and Refunds:
Cancellations received, in writing, fourteen business days prior to the event will be honored. All later cancellations will require a $125 cancellation fee. Cancellations received after March 18, 2009 will not be refunded. Substitutions are permitted with no penalty.

Discounts:
Discounts are offered for the following:

- Early Bird registration with payment received prior to January 17, 2009. See Early Bird pricing below.
- Organizations who send more than four (4) attendees will earn a fifth (5th) registration at no charge.

Online: www.oco.com
Mail: The O'Co
PO Box 17171
New York, NY 10099
Fax: 1-888-999-7777
E-mail: RobbB@oco.com
Phone: 1-800-333-4444
(+1.330.425.9888)

EARLY BIRD SPECIAL

CONFERENCE PACKAGES	Save $$$ by Jan. 17	After Jan. 17
Members		
Pre-conference, conference & trade show	❑ $1,499	❑ $1,599
Conference & trade show only	❑ $1,299	❑ $1,399
Pre-conference only	❑ $499	❑ $599
Non Members (Join and save $100!!)		
Pre-conference, conference & trade show	❑ $1,999	❑ $2,099
Conference & trade show only	❑ $1,799	❑ $1,899
Pre-conference only	❑ $699	❑ $799
Gala Celebration	❑ $100	❑ $125
TOTAL	$________	$________

PAYMENT

❑ Enclosed is my check or money order Check Number:________________
❑ Please charge to the following credit card: ❑VISA ❑MasterCard ❑Discover ❑Am Ex
Account Number:____________________ Expiration Date: ______________
Name (as it appears on card):________________________________
Company Name (as it appears on card):________________________
Cardholder's Signature:______________________________________

REGISTRATION

First Name:____________________ Last Name:____________________
MI:_____ Nickname:____________________ Title:____________________
Company:____
Street Address:_______________________________________
City:________________ State: __________ Zip:__________ Country:__________
Telephone:____________________ Fax:____________________
Email (required for registration confirmation)____________________

If you require special accommodations, please advise us at least two weeks in advance of the event. All requests are kept strictly confidential. We are happy to serve you.

WORKSHOPS

MONDAY, MARCH 21

8:00 AM Continental Breakfast

9:00 AM
❑ Secrets of Power Negotiating
❑ Marketing with the Big Fish
❑ Crossing Intercultural Differences

11:00 AM
❑ Customer Service is Supreme!
❑ Think Like a Marketer
❑ Super Selling

2:30 PM
❑ Global Warming: Heating up your ROI
❑ Accounting for Dummies
❑ Maximizing your Website

4:30 PM Keynote: Tom Matthews
6:00 PM Welcome Reception

TUESDAY, MARCH 22

8:00 AM Continental Breakfast

9:00 AM
❑ Creating a Balance
❑ Pump Up your Volume
❑ Independent Contractors & the IRS

11:00 AM
❑ Hands-on Management
❑ Build Your Business Contacts
❑ Presentations that Win

2:00 PM
❑ Signature Selling
❑ Reinventing Yourself
❑ Government Affairs for the Industry

6:00 PM Awards Ceremony

REGISTERING SPEAKERS

When collecting information from your speakers, you'll be asking much of the same types of information as your attendees, with a few additions. It is recommended that for your convenience, you set up a separate speaker database specifically geared to the information you will need to collect and track.

There are a few types of information that are specific to speakers.

ARRIVAL INFORMATION

It is likely that you will want to track the arrival information for your speakers. You may need to provide transportation from the airport and you may want to be able to follow up with the airlines to make sure the plane arrived safely and on time.

EMERGENCY CONTACT NUMBERS

In addition to the emergency numbers that you ask for from attendees, you'll also want to include a different kind of emergency information for speakers. Should a speaker fail to arrive at the time you expected, you'll want to be able to follow up via a cell phone or with a booking agent. Nearly every seasoned meeting planner has had occasion to worry because with only a couple of hours until the presentation, the speaker had yet to be seen.

SPEAKER PRESENTATION INFORMATION

You will also want to capture and track information about the speakers' presentations. Your speaker database becomes your project management tool. Especially if you're dealing with multiple speakers, you will want an easy-to-use system to keep all the details straight and make sure you have everything you need to produce a successful presentation. This is where you'll track and remind yourself of all the materials you're expecting from the speaker such as their photograph and biography for promotional purposes, their introduction for your emcee and any presentation materials that you're expected to reproduce. Your database will also help you with the room preparation on site. You can track if you'll need an extra table for materials they'd like set out or if they will be doing a book signing after the workshop. You'll also want to remind yourself to get written permission should you want to record or videotape their presentation for future use. Your accounting department will also want you to keep track of how much you've contracted this speaker for and what payment arrangements have been agreed upon.

SPEAKER REQUESTS

It's also critical that you work with your speakers to determine exactly what they will need to give the best presentation possible.

A thorough speaker database management system can help the meeting manager in many ways. First, this process will allow you to gather all the information you need to provide the speaker with exactly what they need to give the best sessions possible. This will help you manage special requests and keep control of costs. It also gives you a tracking system for your correspondence with each speaker. It can serve as a prompt for you to give speakers a reminder to turn in their hotel requests, handout materials or AV requirements.

Will they need data projectors? What kind of mics do they want? Do they have other special needs?

This is important to accomplish early in the process so you can better manage your costs and on-site set up.

For example, rental of a data projector might cost you about $400-$600 per room/per day, each through the hotel's AV department. If you find out that three speakers want to use a projector, you might be able to put them all in one room and save yourself $800. However, if a speaker shows up and wants an extra piece of equipment,

PRESENTATION EQUIPMENT

AUDIO EQUIPMENT

- ❑ Small sound system - 2 sm speakers, mic, 4 ch mixer
- ❑ Medium sound system - 2 med speakers, mic, 6 ch mixer
- ❑ 4 channel audio mixer
- ❑ Wired mic (handheld,headset,lavaliere)
- ❑ Wireless mic (handheld,headset,lavaliere)
- ❑ Small powered speaker (tripod/hanging brackets)
- ❑ CD/Cassette player

VIDEO EQUIPMENT

- ❑ 1/2" VHS player with repeat
- ❑ DVD player
- ❑ BETA SP player with repeat
- ❑ 20" Television
- ❑ 27" Television
- ❑ 32" Television
- ❑ 20" Television/VHS unit
- ❑ 20" VHS/DVD monitor combo
- ❑ 27" VHS/DVD monitor combo
- ❑ 34" Monitor cart w/ skirt
- ❑ 54" Monitor cart w/ skirt

VIDEO/DATA DISPLAY

- ❑ Video/data LCD projector
- ❑ 17" LCD flat screen monitor
- ❑ 20" LCD flat screen monitor
- ❑ 37" Plasma display panel
- ❑ 42" Plasma display panel
- ❑ 50" Plasma display panel
- ❑ 60" Plasma display panel

PROJECTION/SCREENS

- ❑ Overhead projector
- ❑ 5' Tripod screen w/ skirt
- ❑ 6' Tripod screen w/ skirt
- ❑ 7' Tripod screen w/ skirt
- ❑ 6' x 6' Fastfold screen/front w/ skirt
- ❑ 8' x 8' Fastfold screen/front w/ skirt
- ❑ 6' Fastfold
- ❑ 10' Fastfold
- ❑ 12' Fastfold
- ❑ 6' Tripod
- ❑ 7' Tripod
- ❑ 8' Tripod
- ❑ Cradle
- ❑ Roll

COMPUTER SYSTEMS

- ❑ Fixed Lens
- ❑ Flipchart Easel
- ❑ Flipchart Pad
- ❑ Full Range Bi-amp Speaker
- ❑ Laser Pointer
- ❑ Multi-Scan Projector
- ❑ Object Overhead
- ❑ OH Cart
- ❑ Overhead Projector
- ❑ Pointer
- ❑ Portable VHS Camcorder
- ❑ Powered Backstage Monitor Speaker
- ❑ Rear Projection Equipment
- ❑ Speaker With Stand
- ❑ VCR Cart
- ❑ VHS VCR
- ❑ White Boards

Lights

- ❑ Projection
- ❑ Stage Lamps
- ❑ Spotlight
- ❑ Dimmers

COMPUTER PERIPHERALS

- ❑ HP 4000 Series Laserjet Printer
- ❑ HP 5000 Series Laserjet Printer
- ❑ 12 Port ethernet hub
- ❑ 8 Port ethernet hub
- ❑ Keyboard and mouse
- ❑ PC speakers
- ❑ Plain paper fax machine

ELECTRICAL

- ❑ AC Power Extension Cords
- ❑ AC Power Strips With Surge

it will most likely cost more than had you been able to make arrangements ahead of time.

In addition to AV needs, you'll want to work with your speakers in order to know how they'd like their rooms set up. There are a variety of options, each having their own advantages and disadvantages. Become familiar with each type of room set up and learn the benefits of each.

You'll want to work with speakers up front to be able to work with the hotel to make pre-workshop set up as painless and efficient as possible.

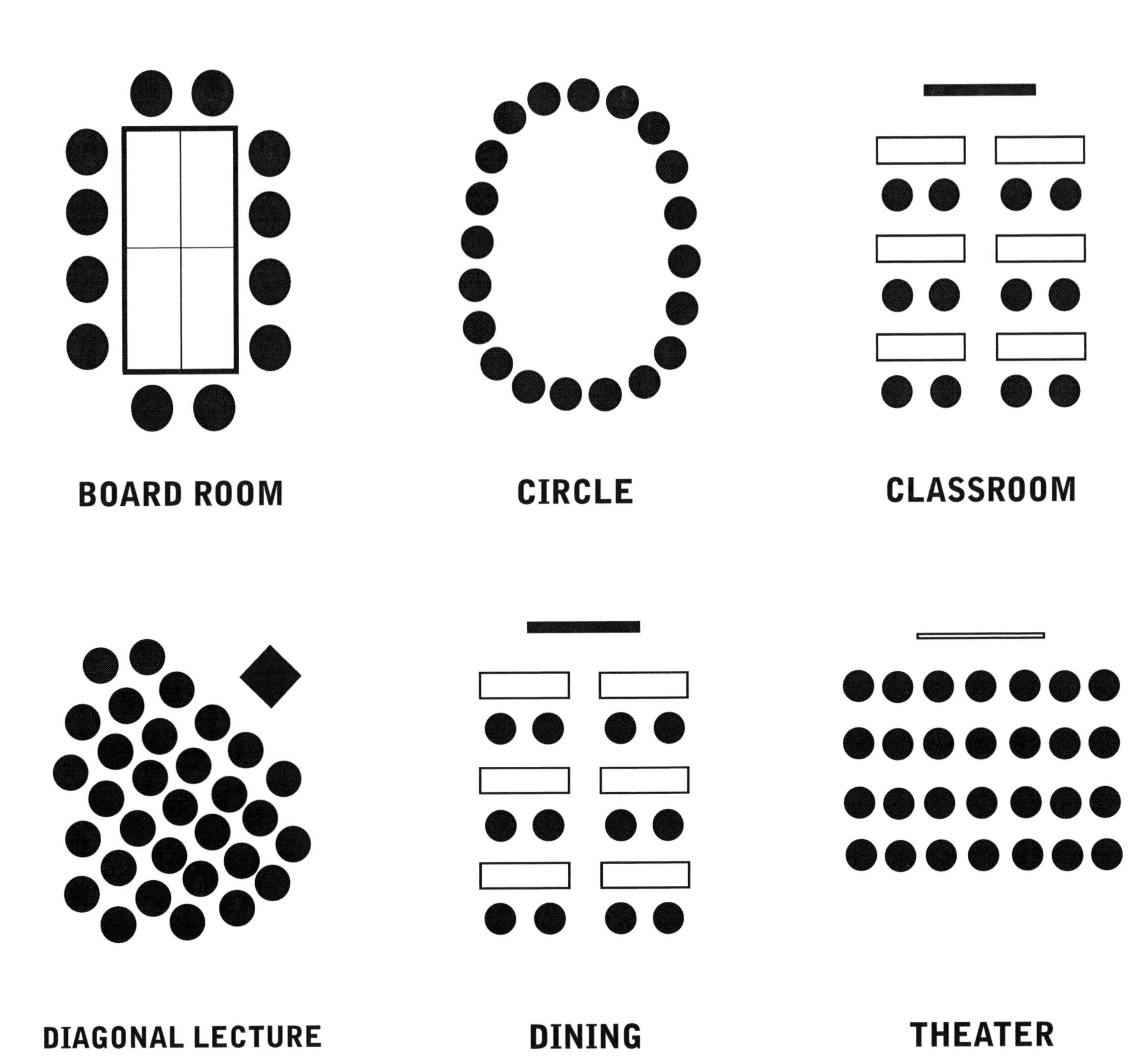

SPEAKER INFORMATION CHECKLIST

PERSONAL INFORMATION
- ❑ Salutation
- ❑ First name
- ❑ Middle initial
- ❑ Last name
- ❑ Badge name
- ❑ Title
- ❑ Organization
- ❑ Address
- ❑ Suite
- ❑ City
- ❑ State
- ❑ Zip code
- ❑ Postal code
- ❑ Country
- ❑ Phone
- ❑ FAX
- ❑ E-mail address

SALUTATION
- ❑ Mr.
- ❑ Ms.
- ❑ Mrs.
- ❑ Dr.
- ❑ Prof.
- ❑ Fr.

SUFFIX
- ❑ B.A. (Bachelor of Arts)
- ❑ M.A. (Master of Arts)
- ❑ M.D. (Medical Doctor)
- ❑ L.L.D. (Doctor of Law)
- ❑ D.D. (Doctor of Divinity)
- ❑ D.D.S. (Doctor of Dental Surgery)
- ❑ B.S. (Bachelor of Science)
- ❑ M.B.A. (Masters of Business Administration)
- ❑ Ph.D. (Doctor of Philosophy)
- ❑ Ed.D. (Doctor of Education)
- ❑ J.D. (Doctor of Jurisprudence)
- ❑ M.E. (Master of Education)
- ❑ Jr.
- ❑ Sr.
- ❑ III

PRESENTER INFORMATION
- ❑ Photo
- ❑ Introduction
- ❑ Handouts
- ❑ Press Release
- ❑ Honorarium amount
- ❑ Advance
- ❑ On-site payment
- ❑ Permission To record
- ❑ Permission To videotape
- ❑ Book Signing
- ❑ Workshop 1
- ❑ Workshop 2
- ❑ Speech 1
- ❑ Speech 2
- ❑ Back-up room name

Arrival Information
- ❑ Arrival date
- ❑ Arrival time
- ❑ Arrival flight
- ❑ Arrival airline
- ❑ Pick-up
- ❑ Taxi
- ❑ Limo
- ❑ Car rental
- ❑ Departure date
- ❑ Departure time
- ❑ Departure flight
- ❑ Departure airline

ROOMING INFORMATION
- ❑ Smoking or non-smoking
- ❑ Late arrival
- ❑ Suite
- ❑ Concierge level
- ❑ Single, double, triple or quad
- ❑ Rate choices
- ❑ Roll-away
- ❑ Suite
- ❑ Studio Suite
- ❑ 1 BR Suite
- ❑ 2 BR Suite
- ❑ VIP Suite
- ❑ Sharing with
  - ❑ ____________________

PRESENTATION EQUIPMENT AUDIO EQUIPMENT
- ❑ Small sound system - 2 sm speakers, mic, 4 ch mixer
- ❑ Medium sound system - 2 med speakers, mic, 6 ch mixer
- ❑ 4 channel audio mixer
- ❑ Wired mic (handheld,headset,lavaliere)
- ❑ Wireless mic (handheld,head set,lavaliere)
- ❑ Small powered speaker (tripod/hanging brackets)
- ❑ CD/Cassette player

VIDEO EQUIPMENT
- ❑ 1/2" VHS player with repeat
- ❑ DVD player
- ❑ BETA SP player with repeat
- ❑ 20" Television
- ❑ 27" Television
- ❑ 32" Television
- ❑ 20" Television/VHS unit
- ❑ 20" VHS/DVD monitor combo
- ❑ 27" VHS/DVD monitor combo
- ❑ 34" Monitor cart w/ skirt
- ❑ 54" Monitor cart w/ skirt

VIDEO/DATA DISPLAY
- ❑ Video/data LCD projector
- ❑ 17" LCD flat screen monitor
- ❑ 20" LCD flat screen monitor
- ❑ 37" Plasma display panel
- ❑ 42" Plasma display panel
- ❑ 50" Plasma display panel
- ❑ 60" Plasma display panel

PROJECTION/SCREENS
- ❑ Overhead projector
- ❑ 5' Tripod screen w/ skirt
- ❑ 6' Tripod screen w/ skirt
- ❑ 7' Tripod screen w/ skirt
- ❑ 6' x 6' Fastfold screen/front w/ skirt
- ❑ 8' x 8' Fastfold screen/front w/ skirt
- ❑ 6' Fastfold
- ❑ 10' Fastfold
- ❑ 12' Fastfold
- ❑ 6' Tripod
- ❑ 7' Tripod
- ❑ 8' Tripod
- ❑ Cradle
- ❑ Roll

COMPUTER SYSTEMS
- ❑ Fixed lens
- ❑ Flipchart easel
- ❑ Flipchart pad
- ❑ Full Range bi-amp speaker
- ❑ Laser pointer
- ❑ Multi-Scan projector
- ❑ Object overhead
- ❑ OH Cart
- ❑ Overhead projector
- ❑ Pointer
- ❑ Portable VHS camcorder
- ❑ Powered backstage monitor speaker
- ❑ Rear projection equipment
- ❑ Speaker with stand
- ❑ VCR cart
- ❑ VHS VCR
- ❑ White boards

LIGHTS
- ❑ Projection
- ❑ Stage lamps
- ❑ Spotlight
- ❑ Dimmers

COMPUTER PERIPHERALS
- ❑ HP 4000 Series Laserjet Printer
- ❑ HP 5000 Series Laserjet Printer
- ❑ 12 Port ethernet hub
- ❑ 8 Port ethernet hub
- ❑ Keyboard and mouse
- ❑ PC speakers
- ❑ Plain paper fax machine

ELECTRICAL
- ❑ AC Power extension cords
- ❑ AC Power strips with surge

ROOM SET-UP
- ❑ U-Shape
- ❑ Square
- ❑ E-Shape
- ❑ Director-board
- ❑ Spoke
- ❑ Classroom
- ❑ Closed tables
- ❑ Herringbone
- ❑ V-Shape
- ❑ Diamond
- ❑ Hexagon
- ❑ Triangle
- ❑ Round
- ❑ Panel set-ups

EMERGENCY CONTACT
- ❑ Name
- ❑ Day phone
- ❑ Night phone
- ❑ Cell phone
- ❑ Relationship

ROOM SET UP

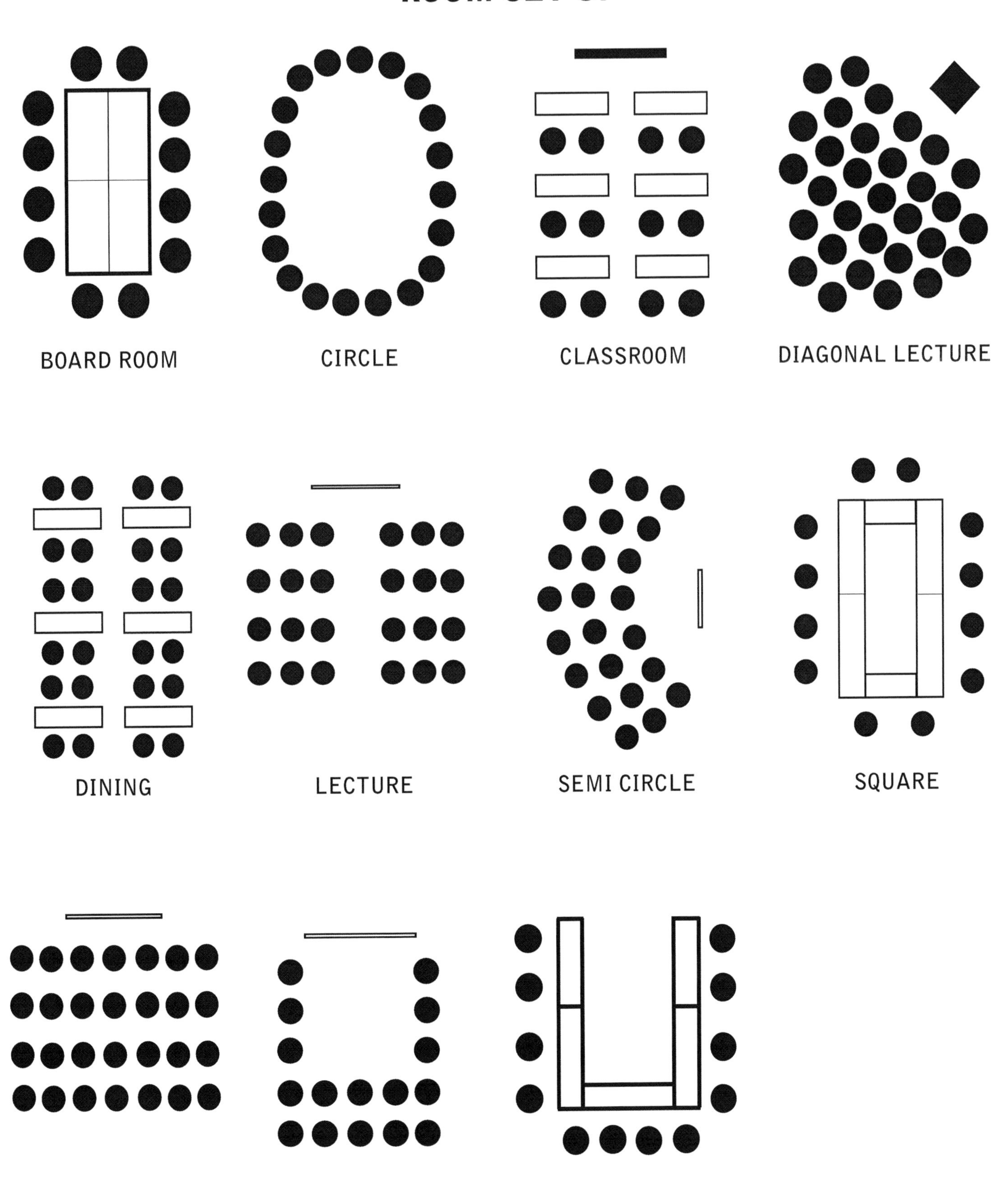
BOARD ROOM
CIRCLE
CLASSROOM
DIAGONAL LECTURE
DINING
LECTURE
SEMI CIRCLE
SQUARE
THEATER
U CHAIRS
U TABLES

THE POWER OF CONFIRMATION

The ability to track and confirm your attendees' and speakers' participation is perhaps one of the most powerful uses for your database.

Remember, until a couple of weeks out, people can cancel. As we've mentioned, tons of reasons pop up at the last minute as to why one shouldn't go to your meeting. It's up to the meeting manager to "make sure they don't change their minds."

ATTENDEES

Confirmation letters are important to keep the attendee enthusiastic about the upcoming experience. They're another chance for selling or rather, re-selling your meeting. You want to use this opportunity to not only verify the information you have is correct, but also to remind the attendees just how much they are looking forward to your meeting.

There are dozens of messages for your confirmation letters. "This is the way your name will appear on your badge. Is it correct?" "We've received your check. Thanks." "Gosh are we looking forward to seeing you in Orlando. Don't forget your suntan lotion!" You can use confirmation letters to inform your attendees about registration times, weather forecasts, special events, appropriate attire, optional events or late-breaking news.

For example, you might want to let your attendees know about a schedule change. One meeting planner used an email blast to inform everyone of a speaker substitution. He felt it important for his meeting's reputation to inform the attendees that the popular key note speaker had cancelled. While no one changed their minds about coming to the conference, everyone was fully informed about the change, so there was no issue on-site.

Depending upon your meeting's needs and your audience, you can send confirmations via e-mail, fax or traditional USPS. However, keep track of which letters you've sent to each attendee in your database. This will help you avoid sending repeats and give you good information for future campaigns.

SPEAKERS

The meeting planner wants to do all he/she can to ensure the speakers all show up and all show up prepared. Confirmation letters are also useful for managing speakers and speakers' commitments.

When a speaker cancels at the last minute, your meeting suffers, you're stuck with all the AV costs and you're likely to be left scrambling trying to fill that spot. Should a speaker show up ill-prepared, it ultimately sheds a negative light on you.

While there are no sure-fire methods to manage speakers' actions, the meeting planner can improve the success rate by creating a solid relationship with each speaker through a series of confirmation letters.

One meeting planner has found this series of letters to be extremely successful and actually applauded by the speakers he works with. He's dubbed his technique the "Chinese Water Torture Method." It goes something like this...

About seven months out he sends the speaker a letter confirming the most basic information, such as the date of the presentation, the subject matter and the compensation arrangements. While this helps the meeting planner double check all the facts, it also serves as a prompt to the speaker to make sure the dates are recorded in his calendar.

Then, several weeks later, he sends another letter inquiring about room set up and AV requirements. Not only is this information important to gather early in the process for planning purposes, it also inspires the speaker to begin thinking about the presentation.

The next letter will ask for speaker materials such as a photo for promotional purposes, press releases to send to the trade publications and hand-out materials for reproduction.

Then, thirty days out, the speaker receives another letter confirming arrival information, hotel reservation and sharing demographic information about the attendees that have signed up for that workshop.

This method keeps your meeting "top-of-mind" for the speaker. It helps promote early preparation and keeps the speaker excited about working with you and your meeting.

Another planner finds it helpful to make a personal call to all speakers 3-5 days prior to the event date to reconfirm session dates and times, and answer any questions.

The registration process is integral to the successful management of a meeting. Remember to visualize the outcome you desire and work backward from there.

The O' Co. The O' Co Conference Management • www.oco.com • 800-717-1717

SAMPLE ATTENDEE CONFIRMATION

January 3, 2009

«name»
«Title»
«Company»
«Mail_Address»
«city_line»

Dear «First_Name»:

We are very pleased you will be attending the 10th Annual Beauty Convention at the Grand Hotel in Orlando, Florida from March 10-14, 2009.

Attached is a copy of your information that will be used for nametags and other materials. We've also included the list of workshops you signed up for.

Please go over the information and let us know by January 31 if any of the information is not correct.

Meanwhile, feel free to visit our website at www.oco.com to check out the variety of local attractions you might want to take in while you're in Orlando.

And it's never too early to start shopping for sunscreen!

I will be mailing additional information as we get closer to the conference. If you have any questions, please feel free to call me at (800) 717-1717.

Sincerely,

Missy Trescher
Conference Coordinator
missytrescher@oco.com
Direct line: (800) 717-1717

August 25, 2009

SAMPLE ATTENDEE CONFIRMATION

Angie Chisholm
Marketing Manager
pc/nametag
3716 Sandia Drive
Plano, TX 75023-6122

Dear Angie:

REGISTRATION NUMBER: 000301

Nicholas Meeting Group is delighted you have chosen to attend our 2009 Professional Education Conference December 11-13, 2009 in Vancouver, Canada. We are the premier educational, technological and peer-interaction resource in the meetings industry. We look forward to welcoming you to beautiful Vancouver!

This letter is your OFFICIAL CONFIRMATION for the conference and badge information.

BADGE INFORMATION

Your badge is necessary for admittance to all Meeting Events. Please notify us in writing, referencing the above registration number, within 10 days ONLY if corrections are needed. For your convenience, the Nicholas Meeting Group fax number is (222) 888-7777. On the basis of your specifications, your badge will read as follows:

ANGIE
Angie Chisholm
pc/nametag
Plano TX

CONFIRMATION OF ADDITIONAL ACTIVITIES (IF APPLICABLE)

We have enclosed additional information that is pertinent to your attendance during the conference. To better serve your on-site needs, please notify our Conference Department by fax or in writing, of any special needs or dietary requirements. For assistance regarding your registration, please contact Elizabeth Tooten at (222) 888-5555 or by fax at (222) 888-7777.

Thank you for your continued support and participation in this critical annual conference. We look forward to seeing you in Vancouver.

Sincerely,

Gary Kaspinage, CMP
Manager of Conferences and Meetings

National Conference on Student Leadership • www.ncslcollege.com • 800-206-4805

«name»
«Title»
«Company»
«Mail_Address»
«city_line»

SAMPLE ATTENDEE FINAL CONFIRMATION

Dear «First_Name»:
The 50th National Conference on Student Leadership is almost here! Below you will find tips to make your conference experience more productive.

Nametags: Check your name, title, school, and email as listed above. This information (name, title & school) will appear on your nametag. If this information is incorrect, indicate changes on this page and fax back to 888-936-4400. Changes submitted by Monday, April 12th will ensure a correct nametag when you arrive! Please remember to wear your nametags to all conference functions.

NCSL Registration: The NCSL registration desk will be located in the Independence Foyer, level 5B of the Grand Hyatt. Registrations are sorted alphabetically BY SCHOOL as most register as groups.

Certified Student Leader (CSL) Program: It's not too late to sign up for the CSL program. The program focuses on developing skills in those areas NCSL has pinpointed as essential for true leaders of any campus organization: parliamentary procedure/meeting skills, diversity/ethics, publicity/budgeting, conflict resolution/communication skills. To become a Certified Student Leader, you must pass the test based on those core workshops. When you pass the test you will be recognized before the entire conference with a special certificate in an award frame. You will receive a Certified Student Leader Pin, a polo shirt, parliamentary procedure pack including a procedure guide and priority sheets. We will also provide a prepared press release for your college paper. On-site registration is $119. You can save $20 by calling in your advance CSL registration by April 5th.

Visit Your Representative!
Join us for an optional trip to the Capitol. Small groups will visit with Senators and Representatives to discuss various proposed bills relating to higher education. We will meet as a group to discuss strategies prior to walking to Capitol. Plan on two to three hours for the visit. To register for this free and informative visit to the Capitol, sign-up in advance on the registration form or call us toll-free at 800-433-0499 by April 5th!

Pre-Conference Optional Program
Democratic Dialogues: The Complexities of Effective Communication, Community Building, and Conflict Resolution on College Campuses (Intended audience: Current Student Affairs Administrators and student leaders aspiring to a career in Student Affairs).
This session, utilizing a participatory approach, is aimed at individuals who wish to establish a shared sense of community and purpose in their organizations and who seek also a repertoire of strategies for effective conflict resolution in varied settings. While a sense of community is imperative to meaningful dialogue, conflict is inevitable on today's college campuses. Through participation in team and trust building activities and through the use of role plays, case studies, and interactive media, participants will engage directly with one another and develop a style of conflict resolution that is reflective of their unique contexts and circumstances. Register for this optional program by April 5, 2009. On-site registration is $89.00 Fax in your optional program registration by April 5th and pay only $69.00. (fax- 888-936-4400).

Transportation:
It is recommended that you make flight arrangements into Ronald Reagan National Airport, the closest airport to the conference hotel, the Grand Hyatt Washington at 1000 H. Street NW, Washington, DC. A 10-15 minute shuttle ride takes you directly to the hotel.

When you arrive at the hotel:
Check in is at 3:00 pm, if your room is not ready you can store your bags at the bell stand.

Schedule of Events:
Explore the NCSL Website at www.ncslcollege.com for complete updates.

We hope these tips prove to be helpful. We look forward to welcoming you to participate in great educational programs at the conference in Washington, D.C.!

Thank you!

National Conference on Student Leadership • www.ncslcollege.com • 800-206-4805

SAMPLE SPEAKER CONFIRMATION #1

January 12, 2009

«name»
«Title»
«Company»
«Mail_Address»
«city_line»

Dear «First_Name»:

We are very pleased you will be a part of the faculty at the 50th National Conference on Student Leadership at the Grand Hyatt Washington in Washington D.C. April 15-18, 2009. Our staff is excited about the conference and we are looking forward to working with you. The attached contract outlines the details of the sessions you will be presenting, compensation package, etc. Please review this form, sign, and fax or mail to me no later than February 9, 2009. If you haven't already submitted it, I will also need a black and white photo for promotional purposes, as well as any revisions to the attached bio and workshop descriptions by February 9, 2009. The session descriptions will appear in the conference promotional mailings as well as website. The bio and session descriptions will appear in the conference program.

I have also attached an audio-visual request form. Please fax or mail to me no later than February 9, 2009. Once we have received all audio-visual requests, we will set session times accordingly. If there is a date or time you would prefer, please indicate preference on audio-visual request. I will do my best to schedule your sessions accordingly.

Our compensation packages differ among faculty based on the following: number of years presenting for NCSS, evaluation scores, number of workshops presented, etc. If you have a question about your compensation package, please call me at 608-777-7777.

Speakers are responsible for calling the hotel and making their lodging reservations. Please let them know that you are a speaker for NCSL. They will most likely ask for a credit card number to confirm your reservation. The number at the Grand Hyatt Washington is 202-582-1234. Call soon, as the hotel is sure to fill up quickly!

I will be mailing additional information as we get closer to the conference. If you have any questions, please feel free to call me at (608) 777-7777.

Sincerely,

MaryAnn Mlekush
Conference Coordinator
mmlekush@magnapubs.com
Direct line: 608/777-7777

National Conference on Student Leadership • www.ncslcollege.com • 800-206-4805

SAMPLE SPEAKER CONFIRMATION #2

February 17, 2009

«name»
«Title»
«Company»
«Mail_Address»
«city_line»

Dear «First_Name»:

Only 7 weeks until the 50th National Conference on Student Leadership at the Grand Hyatt in Washington D.C.! We certainly value all the time and effort you put into your workshop(s) and hope you will find it rewarding.

Please Note: Attached you will find your confirmed session(s), times/AV needs. Please check your session date/time and AV requests. Call me by February 27th if there is any conflict, or if AV needs are not recorded correctly.

Exhibit and Faculty/Showcase Mingle: From 4:00pm-5:00pm on Thursday, April 15th. We will have an informal area for faculty members to mingle with participants. Each faculty member will have 1/6th of a 6 ft table for placement of literature. It will be a great opportunity to meet participants, and promote your talents. Selling of books, videos, etc. will be allowed – however faculty is responsible for obtaining and completing appropriate tax forms. You are responsible for handling of all transactions, etc. Please let me know if you are participating so I can ensure appropriate space.

Literature Resource Table: All faculty members are welcome to place promotional materials/extra handouts at the NCSL resource table. Please bring between 200-300 quantity. Size is limited to 8-1/2 x 11 space (can be packet, etc).

Faculty Reception: Please plan on joining us Thursday, April 15th from 6:00pm-7:00pm for our faculty/partner reception. It's a great way to mingle with fellow faculty as well as NCSL Partnership members. It also allows NCSL staff an opportunity to show our appreciation for your outstanding faculty efforts. We hope you can join us! Spouses/significant others are also welcome to attend. Please let me know if you plan on bringing a guest. Location will be provided on-site.

If you haven't already made your hotel reservation, we urge you to do so as soon as possible, as the hotel will be sure to fill up quickly! Please call the hotel directly at 202-582-1234. Please let them know you are a speaker for NCSL.

If you have any questions please don't hesitate to let me know!

Sincerely,

MaryAnn Mlekush
Conference Coordinator
mmlekush@magnapubs.com
Direct line: 608/777-7777

National Conference on Student Leadership • www.ncslcollege.com • 800-206-4805

SAMPLE SPEAKER CONFIRMATION #3

March 26, 2009

«name»
«Title»
«Company»
«Mail_Address»
«city_line»

Dear NCSL Faculty:

The conference is almost here - just three weeks away! I hope you are looking forward to it as much as we are. Our registration counts are continuing to increase. Anticipated attendance is around 450.

NCSL Registration will open at 9:00 am on Thursday, April 15, 2009 located in the Independence Foyer on level 5B of the Grand Hyatt in Washington D.C. Please stop by the registration area to pick up your faculty badge, conference materials, etc.

Opening keynote, The Logic of Success by Victor Gonzalez will start at 1 pm on Thursday followed by Courage, Caring & Collaboration: How Students & Administrators Create the Future of Higher Education by Dr. Luoluo Hong. Immediately following Courage, Caring & Collaboration we will have an informal area set up by registration for faculty members to mingle with participants. Each speaker (who requests space) will have 1/6th of a 6ft table for placement of literature, etc. It will be a great opportunity to meet participants, and promote your talents. Selling of books, videos, etc. will be allowed – however faculty is responsible for obtaining and completing appropriate tax forms. You are responsible for handling of all transactions, etc. Please let me know if you will be participating by April 2nd so we have appropriate space/signage available for you.

We would like to remind you of the faculty/partner reception on Thursday, April 15th from 6:00 – 7:00 pm (Location to be determined). This is a great opportunity to meet fellow faculty members. It also allows NCSL staff an opportunity to show our appreciation for your outstanding faculty efforts. We hope you can join us! Spouses/significant others are also welcome to attend. Please let me know if you plan on bringing a guest.

I've also attached our Faculty Expectations. In it you will find tips and reminders to help make this a successful event. Please take the time to review these items before your presentation.

If there is anything we can do between now and the conference, please don't hesitate to call. Carrie and I will be leaving for Washington D.C. early on the 13th of April. After that point, we can be reached at the Grand Hyatt 202-582-1234 if there is an emergency you may call my cell phone at 608-888-8888.

Sincerely,

MaryAnn Mlekush
Conference Coordinator
mmlekush@magnapubs.com
Direct line: 608/777-7777

THE ALL IMPORTANT NAMETAG

The nametag is probably the single most significant item for a meeting planner.

Meetings, conventions and trade shows are all about networking. For graceful and effective networking, nametags are key. Nametags are powerful ice breakers. They shatter barriers of unfamiliarity and bouts of shyness with the instant courage of knowing another's first name. For attendees, effective nametags can mean the difference between making new connections and needed contacts or having a lousy time at your event.

But the importance of nametags doesn't stop there. In most meetings, nametags are often used as entry into your convention, special seminar, gala event or confidential sales meeting. Essentially, they're a form of currency, worth anywhere between a couple of bucks to a couple thousands of dollars. Not to mention, millions' worth in company secrets.

Nametags come in all levels of quality from the top-of-the-line metallic permanent engraved nametag to the simplest paper adhesive "Hello my name is…."

Before making their selections, good meeting planners will consider the needs of the audience and the objectives of the meeting. A short meeting of familiar Board Members will suggest different nametag choices than would a week long trade show with many suppliers and potential buyers. The savvy meeting planner will also consider how to protect the valuable nametags and reduce the ability to duplicate them for unauthorized access.

WHAT'S IN A NAMETAG?

These are some of the elements you'll need to consider when selecting your nametags

1. Nametag Inserts
2. Nametag Holders
3. Fastener Systems
4. Deluxe Embellishments

You'll soon discover that there are just about as many nametag options as there are types of attendees that could show up for your program. The most traditional nametags include a paper insert and a vinyl holder, however, there are a few that don't fit these specifications.

TRADITIONAL NAMETAGS

Traditional nametags include a paper insert and a plastic nametag holder. Options in this category are multitudinous. One can choose between plain white stock or a variety of paper color options, select from a variety of sizes, pick from an assortment of holders, embellish their nametags with a fastener or necklace of their choice, and do as much of the work as he or she wants.

PAPER INSERTS

Most paper inserts are white, but some suppliers offer different colored paper stocks. Most meeting planners opt to start out with white inserts and add color through their logo, meeting design, tinted holders or accessory ribbons that come in a rainbow of colors, and display a multitude of various messages.

Common Nametag Sizes

The most common sizes for nametags are: 4" x 3", 4" x 2.5", 4.25" x 3" and 3.5" x 2.25". These standards are complimented by holders in each size. While the most popular 4" x 3" size will comfortably accommodate 4 lines of type, many suppliers suggest inching up to the 4.25" x 3" size to give a bit more room for information and branding. As this larger size does not have side margins, there's less tearing for the meeting planner to do. As one gets closer to meeting time, every corner cut counts! Remember, however, this larger size does require a special complementary holder.

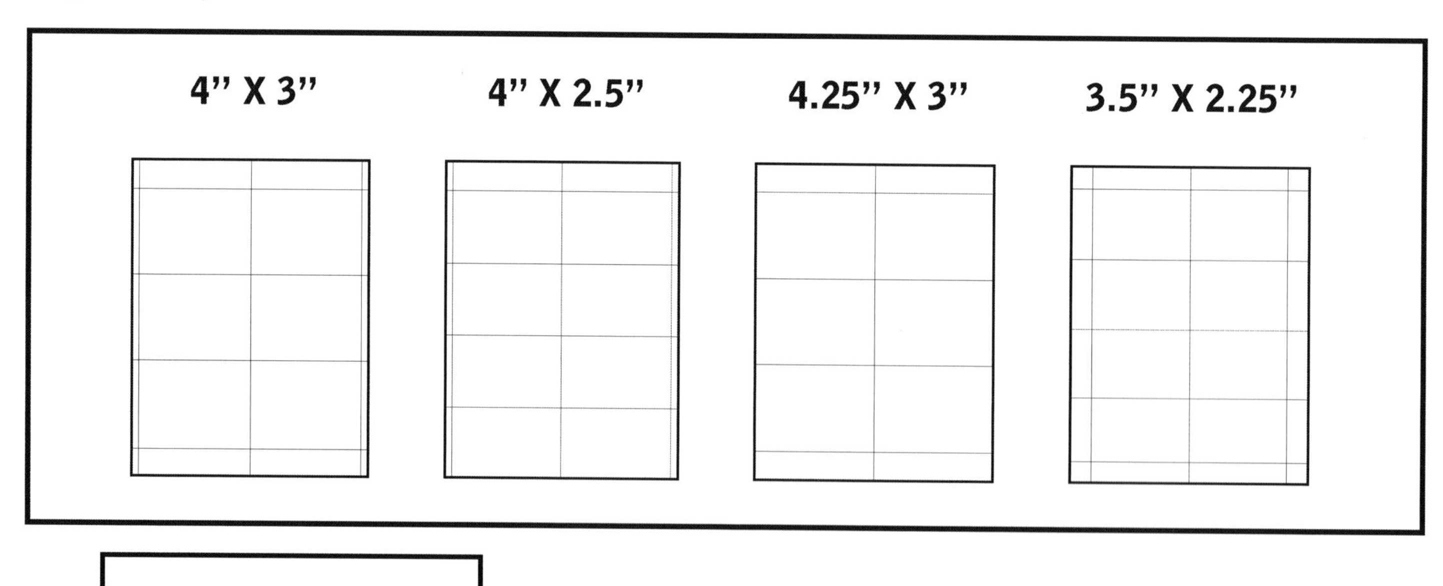

The smaller 3.5" x 2.25" are often used for formal events or international events. In Europe, for example, smaller, more formal nametags are much more acceptable than the larger ones displaying attendees' first names in huge 40 point type, such as is preferred in the U.S.

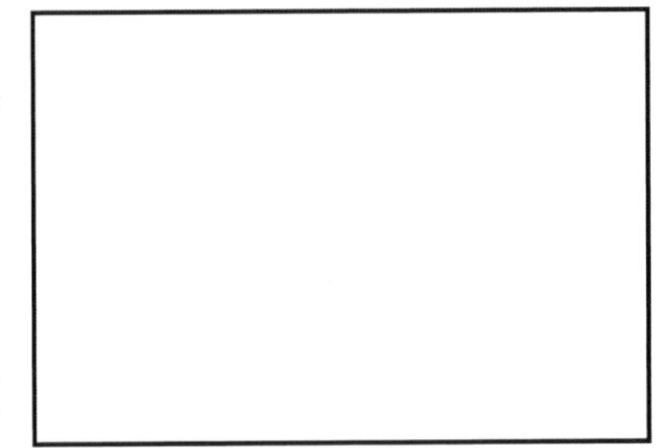

To accommodate three or four lines of type, you'll want to go with either the 4" x 3" or slightly larger 4.25" x 3". For two lines, you can move down to the 4" x 2.5" size. If you are going with the more formal 3.5" x 2.25", you will only be able to use two lines of type.

If, for whatever reason, none of these sizes suits your needs, most nametag suppliers will offer customized inserts and holders for your convenience.

Since most tags don't fit perfectly on an 8.5" x 11" sheet of paper, you will have to anticipate some waste. Once you choose the size you want, you will need to make sure your computer program supports the layout you're purchasing before you order.

When making your selection, ask your printer for the micro-perforated option. These nametags are made with very tiny perforations which are placed very close together. The less expensive, regular perforations can actually harm your laser printer's drum. In addition, the micro-perforated badge stock makes it easier to tear and eliminates the tell-tale jagged edges that come with some cheaper versions.

TIP:
Always use perforated badge stock. Typical 20-pound copy paper is too flimsy and too difficult to stuff. Hand cutting with scissors or knife takes forever and almost always looks homemade.

TIP:
When tearing apart perforated badges, bend at the perforation three times back and forth. This will make it easier to pull the badges apart. You can bend and tear up to five sheets at a time, but remember doing so will throw off your alphabetization. Simply re-alphabetize as you go along.

TIP:
Don't use index cards. They look tacky and are nearly impossible to run through a laser printer!

JUMBO, "BACK STAGE PASS-STYLE" NAMETAG SIZES

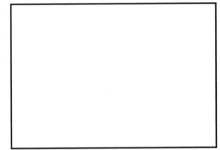

In recent years, larger format and vertical nametags have taken on immense popularity. These formats allow nametags to carry more visual impact, more information, more branding and more kudos for sponsors. In addition, the increased real estate on the back side of the name badge affords meeting planners a spacious placard for publishing the meeting agenda or other critical information. Vertical nametags have become especially popular for music or sporting events.

Recently, meeting planners have adopted this orientation when they're throwing a special event or one that is intended to mimic these other types of events. Verticals are also often used for employee IDs and badges.

Remember when choosing a vertical nametag, you will most likely want to choose a necklace or lanyard instead of a pin or clip. With the exception of the petite 2.25" x 3.5" version, most verticals will look strange on a breast pocket or lapel as they are just too long.

Design Options

Many meeting planners opt for preprinted badge stock sporting their branding and logo. Suppliers offer expert printing and art services to ensure a professional look that reinforces the branding. Depending upon the objectives and the budget, a meeting planner can choose from one-color to four-color printing. Remember that when working with an outside printer, larger runs are most cost effective, so order extras from the onset. It's easy to rack up a lot of cost ordering extras at the last minute.

Off-the-shelf options are another alternative for meeting planners who want to add color and organization to their meetings. Meeting supply companies offer many choices from color-banded badges (to help distinguish those that have paid for the full conference verses those that have only paid for a day or two) or titled nametags (to identify who's a speaker, an exhibitor, an attendee or a Board member).

These types of identification systems not only make it easier for the attendees to network more effectively, but also help the meeting planner keep track of who's who and who should be where. These off-the-shelf badges are very cost effective for even small quantities.

NON-TRADITIONAL NAMETAGS

HIGH-END NAMETAGS

High-end nametags are perfect for recurring gatherings, annual events, staff identification, VIP acknowledgement and black-tie events or for making a particularly good first impression.

Options in this nametag category include customized rigid badges, credit card-like badges and engraved nametags. Customized rigid badges can lend impact and powerful branding to any event. This technique accommodates full-color graphics and customized die cuts to complement the event theme.

The credit card-like badge allows for full-color graphics and two-sided imprinting for a bar code or special message. These lend an air of quality, are convenient to store in a wallet and are especially good for recurring functions such as monthly meetings.

Permanent engraved nametags are perfect for black-tie events and exude a polished, professional image. They are also excellent for repeated use.

All nametags in this category also afford the busy meeting planner another benefit. As they are either printed or engraved, there is no need for a holder and therefore no extra work. There's no perforating, no stuffing and no assembly whatsoever.

TIP:

When using either printed or engraved nametags, order a few extras without names. Using clear labels and a laser printer, you can make corrections or additions on site with nearly the same high-end look.

BUDGET NAMETAGS

At the lowest end of the price spectrum, there are more non-traditional choices. The pressure-sensitive stick-on nametag falls into this category. This option is often used for short or informal meetings. However, there is a drawback with this type of nametag. Many people object to placing them on their clothing as the adhesive can damage fine fabrics, leave a stubborn residue or fail to stick.

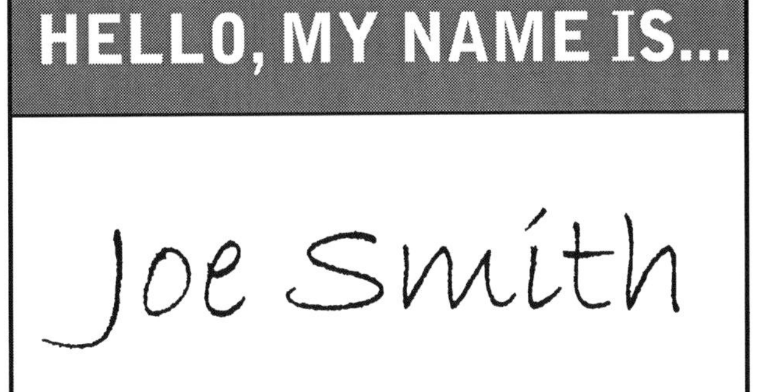

Pre-perforated badge stock is now available for pressure-sensitive nametags. This allows the meeting planner to run the badges through a desktop printer, lending a bit more professionalism, and then the ability to tear them apart without removing the backing. This makes for a much more organized registration process as the badges can be sorted or inserted into registration packages ahead of time.

The newest member of the non-traditional nametag family is the paper-only nametag. These are made of heavier stock that runs through a basic laser or ink jet printer. Because the stock is heavy enough, there is no need for the additional expense of a holder. After printing, a fastener is affixed to the back of the tag. This option doesn't save the meeting planner a whole lot of time, but does eliminate the need to purchase a separate holder, usually saving a bit of money.

YOU CAN NEVER BE TOO CAREFUL

1. *Insist on laser-safe ink.*

   When working with a vendor to provide pre-printed badge stock, make certain you will be receiving materials printed with laser-safe inks. If your stock isn't laser-safe, it could produce toxic fumes and/or damage your laser printer when you run it through to add your personalized information.

2. *Keep your badge stock protected.*

   For most meeting planners, nametags are just like currency. Make certain you have made arrangements to keep extra badge stock and unclaimed nametags under lock and key.

3. *Use your design as your protection.*

   Don't reuse the same badge stock design year after year, making it too easy for an attendee to save theirs from last year to avoid paying for this one. Also remember, it's harder to duplicate a customized or preprinted insert. In addition to the important branding, customized designed inserts add an element of security.

DON'T FORGET THE BACK!

Many meeting planners make the mistake of wasting the precious space on the back of a nametag. Think about it. The back of a nametag provides a highly visible, blank canvas for a wide variety of messages. This space can be leveraged to help realize a whole host of meeting objectives from information dissemination to sponsor visibility.

1. Agenda

The back of a nametag is a perfect place to provide attendees with an easy-reference short list of the main agenda items and locations.

Thursday, November 13

8:00 - 8:30	Continental Breakfast - Salon A
8:30 - 5:00	General Session - Salon B
12:00 - 1:30	Lunch - Poolside
6:00 - 7:00	Reception - The Crystal Room

Friday, November 14

8:00 - 8:30	Continental Breakfast - Salon A
8:30 - Noon	General Session - Salon B

2. On-location emergency information

As being away from home can be stressful for some, give your attendees added security by providing them with important emergency numbers such as police, fire, ambulance, the nearest emergency room, as well as local support groups such as Alcoholics and Gamblers Anonymous.

Medical Conditions ____________

Allergies ____________

Emergency Contact:
Name ____________

Phone ____________

Cell ____________

3. Personal emergency information

The back of a nametag can also be used as a safety precaution. Use this space to offer lines where attendees could list medical conditions such as diabetes, epilepsy or the existence of a pace maker.

In addition, consider offering space for attendees to list their personal emergency contact information, in case of an accident.

4. Sponsorship advertising

This valuable real estate can also be considered for sponsor investment. The back of a nametag, which provides excellent visibility, is an often overlooked advertising opportunity. Sell sponsorship of your nametags with the benefit of having the sponsor's name and logo displayed as "Nametags brought to you by ACME Company." Alternatively, consider offering this advertising space to sponsors to give them more exposure for their logo.

5. Meeting promotion

It's a well known meeting planning fact that the best time to start marketing next year's event is at this year's. Use the back of the nametag to "Save the date for next year's Annual Conference" or to offer discounts for other upcoming events, "Present this badge for 10% off our Spring Seminar."

6. Maps

Maps can be a very helpful benefit to meeting attendees who are in unfamiliar territory. Consider mapping out the local area—perfect for locations such as New Orleans, where everyone wants to know how to get around Bourbon Street. Or displaying the layout of the trade show floor—especially if you're hosting a large trade show. In fact, sometimes it's even helpful to offer a map of the hotel. In Las Vegas, for example, hotels are massive and can be quite confusing. Maps can also be helpful for corporate events in a public venue, say at the zoo or a music festival, where your event will be surrounded by thousands of general admission attendees.

7. Local retailer advertising

Local advertising is another creative use for the back of a nametag. Neighboring retailers might be looking for a bit of added business during your meeting. Offer the back of your nametags as valuable advertising space to nearby restaurants or store fronts. They make great limited time coupons or warm invitations.

Looking for an authentic Mexican Meal?

We're

La Cocina Restaurante

and we're right next door!

Present this badge for 20% off all meals through Friday, May 17th

8. Local phone listings

When people are out of their element, they are often grateful to have some of the comforts of home readily accessible. List local conveniences that might make an attendee's stay a bit more comfortable. These might include: cab companies, nearby theaters, restaurants, take-out delivery, churches or temples, dry cleaners, office supply stores and quick printers.

9. Registration information

If there is a meeting hotline, be sure to list it on the back of the nametag. This is also a good place to list the hours of the registration counter.

10. Quote of the day

Finally, the back of the nametag is a perfect place for you to reinforce the message of the meeting. Consider listing the company's mission statement, highlights from the keynote speaker or photos of the new product line.

PRINTING NAMES ON INSERTS

Another consideration while ordering nametags is how you are going to print the personalized names on each. Again, there are many options available, from doing it all yourself to outsourcing the entire task.

Some planners use a common software, such as Microsoft® Word to create their nametags. As most people are familiar with this program and as it integrates well with a database set up in Microsoft® Excel, it can be a cost-effective solution. However, it's important to be aware that the cost savings can quickly be eaten up by the time it takes to produce nametags without a program specifically designed to do so. Usually, this method is only reasonable for small meetings when less than 50 nametags are required.

When using Microsoft® Word as your nametag program, remember that it was not set up to automatically adjust the font size to accommodate longer names. As the names are merged into the nametag template, long names will wrap onto the next line of text, throwing off all information following it. Before beginning to print, remember to scroll through the entire document to make adjustments by hand and to ensure everything lines up correctly. Lots of ink, paper stock and time can be wasted if one doesn't catch the mistake before starting to print! Also, factor in the "hidden" costs such as labor and ink. These days, color printers might be inexpensive, but the ink is often very pricey.

To cut down on lost time and resources, many meeting planners invest in a specialized software. These range in price from a minimum cost of $50 for software that simply creates nametags to $300-plus for software that also handles all aspects of the registration process to complete meeting software that integrates into the company's accounting and data base programs. These fully-integrated programs start at upwards of thousands of dollars.

Here is an analysis of three options for the creation of 500 nametags, using a two-color imprint (one color plus black) on plain 4"x 3" stock and vinyl holders with clips. For labor costs we've chosen a mid-range salary of $49,000/year. Without benefits, this comes to approximately $24.00/hour. Of course, hourly wages could be much greater or much lower, depending upon who will be actually doing the work. See the "Nametag Toolbox" for an empty table for you to use.

	Do it all yourself		Order imprinted nametags and personalize them.		Completely out-source	
Database set up and input— 50 records per hour	10 hrs	$240	10 hrs	$240	10 hrs	$240
Research various options	2 hrs	$48	2 hrs	$48	.5 hrs	$12
Go to office supply store	2 hrs	$48				
Off-the-shelf nametag kits (100/kit)	6@ $70.00	$420				
Nametag inserts (2-c imprint)			600	$174		
Vinyl holders with clip			600	$186		
Nametag software*	1 program*	$50	1 program*	$50		
Nametag design and set up	8 hrs	$192	4 hrs	$96		
Printing (85 pages)	3 hrs/color+bk	$72	1hr/black	$24		
Assembly	7 hrs	$168	7 hrs	$168		
Alphabetizing	2 hrs	$48	2 hrs	$48		
Organizing Case for Shipping	5 sets	$63	5 sets	$63		$25
Shipping				$25		
500 2-color nametags, printed, assembled, alphabetized and shipped +100 extras					600 sets	$846
TOTAL	**34 hrs**	**$1,348**	**26 hrs**	**$1,121**	**10.5 hrs**	**$1,123**

**$50 software for simply printing nametags, or more expensive meeting software amortized over several meetings.*

For some meeting planners, outsourcing the entire job can be the most cost-effective option, or even worth the extra expense, to free themselves up to handle other details. Carefully weigh all the factors in your particular situation to determine which way is the best for you.

Design considerations for personalizing your nametags

Choose a simple, easier to read font. Most likely you will want to use a sans serif font such as Arial or Helvetica. As you want your attendees to be able to read others' first names from at least ten feet away, it's important to use a large enough font. Experts recommend the following type sizes:

Most important information: 26 to 40 points
Next most important information: 20-24 points
Tertiary information: 18-20 points

**Try to use a software that automatically condenses names.*

NAMETAG HOLDERS

When using a traditional nametag system, your next decision will be which holder you will choose to house your precious badges.

Vinyl

By far, the most popular nametag holder is vinyl. Vinyl gives the impression of higher quality, is softer and is much easier to load. There is little chance with a good quality vinyl holder of cracking or ripping during a several day conference.

Vinyl holders come in a variety of styles and colors with optional embellishments for easy identification and customization. As vinyl holders are sturdy and typically top loading, they also offer attendees a convenient storage option for room keys, extra business cards or tickets behind their nametags.

However, vinyl—especially cheap vinyl—can warp and take on the shape it's stored in. To prevent this from happening, store your badges flat in a climate similar to that which you'd like. Not too hot. Not too cold. Not too humid. Vinyl also tends to yellow over time. If you're using vinyl holders over and over, say for a local chapter that holds monthly meetings, they'll need to be replaced every six months or so.

Rigid Vinyl

The more economical rigid vinyl holders are especially useful for budget meetings. Rigid vinyl is harder and has sharper edges compared to vinyl, but has a longer shelf life. However, they must be stored in a cool, dark, covered area in order to protect their quality. Since most rigid vinyl holders are side loading, badges can occasionally fall out.

Lamination

Lamination provides a quality upgrade to nametag holders with permanent protection. Not only do laminated badges appear to be that much more valuable, they also make it very difficult for free-loaders to forge and sneak into where they don't belong.

Laminated badges are also excellent solutions for repeated use, say for monthly chapter meetings for churches or professional clubs, and will last for years.

There are a variety of lamination techniques that allow for in-house and on-site nametag creation. This will take meeting planners longer, because after placing the badge into the plastic material, they'll have to run it through the lamination machine and then attach the clip. However, the perceived high quality may well be worth the effort. One can purchase a lamination machine or look to an outsourcing company for this service.

Sizing up your holder

Be careful to order the proper holders for the size of inserts you order. Some manufacturers name the size of the holder by the actual size of the plastic, others name theirs by the size of the insert it carries. Be sure always to verify with your meeting supplier to be certain the inserts you choose actually fit into the holder!

GET A HOLD ON YOUR NAMETAGS

Traditional Fasteners

Pins

The pin fastener is the least expensive choice. However, it might not be used by those who don't wish to harm their clothing. This is not as important for a casual sporting event, such as a golf outing where the clothing won't be as delicate as the silks and rayons of a business meeting. However, at a formal corporate or black tie event, this could be an issue. If attendees won't wear their nametags, the networking effectiveness will decrease, sponsorship exposure will decline and all of that will leave a negative impression of you.

Clips

Clip fasteners on the other hand, won't harm clothing. But, they won't attach easily without a collar or lapel. This could pose a problem in a casual setting where people are wearing crew-necks and turtle necks or at a black tie affair where women are wearing spaghetti straps and off-the- shoulder gowns. However, you can solve this problem by offering the option of a necklace.

Combos

Many meeting planners purchase the "combo" option, giving their attendees the choice of either a pin or a clip. Giving your attendees a choice is always perceived as a benefit. For a couple more cents, offering alternatives can make you look like a hero. Combo clips are even more important for multi-day or multi-function events as they quickly convert to accommodate the jacket lapel for the workshops as well as the golf shirt for the outing or the strapless gown for the gala.

Magnet Fasteners

The "magnet attachment" is a twist on the traditional fastener. A magnet is attached to the back of the nametag and is secured onto the participant with another magnet behind his or her clothing. This is the highest choice and is most impressive to attendees. There's no risk to clothing and can be attached to most anything your attendees are wearing. If you choose this option, however, be sure to order extras for the attendee that loses one half of his/her magnet fastener. It's important to note that magnets may interfere with the performance of pacemakers and items with magnetic information such as credit cards, room keys and diskettes. Always have some traditional clasps on hand for those that can't or don't want to use magnets.

FROM THE FIELD...

"We use 8.5 x 11 perforated laser badge stock with 6 badges per page. This idea uses twice as much stock, but I think it's worth it. When we set up our badges to print, we set up 2 sections for each attendee. On the left side we print the normal "front of the badge" info such as name, title, company. On the right side we print that person's emergency info: allergies, medical conditions, emergency contact, etc. So we're basically only printing 3 people per page of badges. We leave the 2 sections connected and just fold them in half and insert into the badge holder. That way, in case of emergency, all anyone has to do is flip around the person's badge and their emergency info is right there—no delays while we find someone to access the registration database and get emergency contact info. We haven't had to use it yet, but seems like a good precaution just in case."

MM, CMP

"Nothing is more frustrating than when a customer comes to the booth and the person they would like to see has gone for a walk.

I solved this problem by making small laminated cards with all of our on-site staff's names and phone numbers on them. Then, I put them behind their badges in the badge holders. They never lose it because you always need the badge to be in the exhibit hall. When an important customer arrives to the booth looking for someone, we can easily get on our cell and track him/her down in a hurry."

MW
Marketing Specialist
Camtronics Medical Systems

"This may seem trivial to you seasoned planners but may be helpful to those new to the industry. We use the 4"x4" inserts and matching holders for our name tags. I now print on the back of the name tag a brief agenda with meeting room names and times so the attendees have a quick reference. I have received so many positive comments on this. It truly helps your registrants and makes you look efficient. Don't forget to mention it when they register. They are no longer wandering around the hotel looking for a reader board to point them in the right direction. It is also helpful in getting the events started on time.

THURSDAY, NOVEMBER 13
8:00 - 8:30 Continental Breakfast - Salon A
8:30 - 5:00 General Session - Salon B
12:00 - 1:30 Lunch - Poolside
6:00 - 7:00 Reception - The Crystal Room

FRIDAY, NOVEMBER 14
8:00 - 8:30 Continental Breakfast - Salon A
8:30 - Noon General Session - Salon B

I also give a copy to the hotel so they can print the daily reader boards. This is another reminder and an exact copy of what the registrants see to ensure the reader boards are printed correctly. I know this seems like such a small item, however, we all know how frustrating it is when small details turn into big issues. Ever tried getting a reader board corrected at 7:00 am? Most hotel staff doesn't arrive until 8:00 and my meeting has already started. Unfortunately, I do not have the benefit of having other staff members to assist me on-site. I am the only planner for my company and the only contact on-site for the hotel and registrants. Something as minor as this can take valuable time away from my other responsibilities."

KB
Meeting Coordinator
NCIF

"DO IT YOURSELF" COST COMPARISON GRID

	Do it all yourself		Order imprinted nametags and personalize them.		Completely outsource	
Database set up and input—(50 records per hour)	hrs	$	hrs	$	hrs	$
Research various options	hrs	$	hrs	$	hrs	$
Go to office supply store	hrs	$	hrs	$	hrs	$
Off-the-shelf nametag kits	@	$	@	$	@	$
Nametag inserts	$	$	$	$	$	$
Vinyl holders with clip	$	$	$	$	$	$
Nametag software	$	$	$	$	$	$
Nametag design and set up	hrs	$	hrs	$	hrs	$
Printing	hrs	$	hrs	$	hrs	$
Assembly	hrs	$	hrs	$	hrs	$
Alphabetizing	hrs	$	hrs	$	hrs	$
Organizing Case for Shipping	$	$	$	$	$	$
Shipping	$	$	$	$	$	$
2-color nametags, printed, assembled, alphabetized and shipped +100 extras	**hrs**		**hrs**		**hrs**	
TOTAL		**$**		**$**		**$**

POPULAR NAMETAG SIZES

4" X 3"

- The most popular size nametag, accounting for nearly 80% of all nametags sold.
- Can comfortably accommodate up to four lines of type.

SPEAKER

Maggie
Maggie Miller
Assistant Buyer
Bill's Book House

4.25" X 3"

- The newest addition to the nametag badge stock size.
- Allows a bit more room for important information.
- Saves valuable time as there are no side margins to tear off.
- Can comfortably accommodate up to four lines of type.

ANASTASIA

Anastasia Beltsos
Lead Baker & Designer
Beltsos Bakery and Confections

4" X 2.5"

- A combination of American and International styles.
- Can comfortably accommodate up to three lines of type.

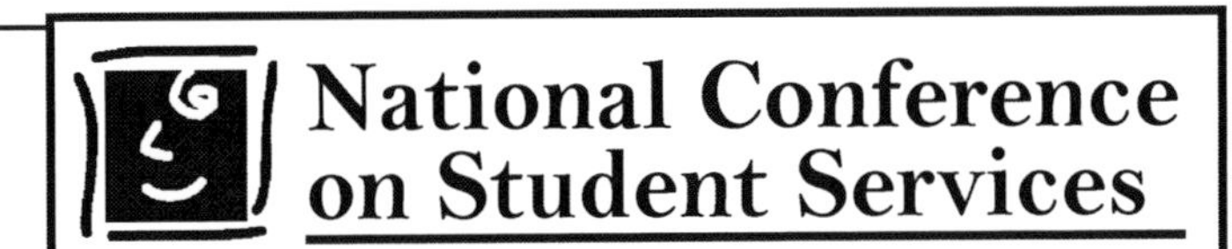

JUDITH
JUDITH EMMONS
SCREENING COMMITTEE

POPULAR NAMETAG SIZES #2

3.5" X 2.5"

- A more elegant size nametag appropriate for formal events
- Most common size for overseas conferences
- Can comfortably accommodate two lines of type

Allie Emmons

Manager

"BACK STAGE PASS" STYLE

- The most current trend in name badges are the oversized, vertical format version that resembles a back stage pass
- Especially good for special events and conferences designed for the younger audiences
- These nametags carry more visual impact, more information, more branding and more kudos for

sponsors.

- Vertical name badges come in a variety of sizes, from 2" x 3" to 4" x 8" to accommodate as much branding and information as you'd like.

Communications Manager

EVENT STAFF

THE ANATOMY OF A WELL-DESIGNED NAMETAG

Use the '10 Foot Rule' for the nametags' type size. Make sure the wearer's first name (or nickname) is readable from 10 feet

Use your logo or meeting theme. Including these graphic elements on nametags lends continuity to your message

Most important information at least **26 to 40 points.**

Next most important information at least **20 to 24 points.**

Tertiary information at least **18 to 20 points.**

pc/nametag®

JOHN

John Chisholm

pc/nametag

MARKETING

VIP

SPEAKER

Use a first name or nickname on the nametag. This encourages a comfortable level of familiarity at your meeting. Plus, these names are typically shorter, making them easy to see and read in large type.

The attendee's first name or nickname is the most critical information and should be set in the largest size type.

Use easy-to-read type

Most experts suggest using a sans serif type (a straight font without "little feet") such as:

- Helvetica
- Arial
- Arial Narrow
- Futura
- Avant Garde
- **Univers**

These fonts tend to be more legible for short use as on a name badge or as a headline.

Consider color contrast. The most legible color combinations are black on yellow or black on white. Obviously, pairing dark pink lettering on a light red background would not be very visible across a crowded room.

Keep the type large and uncrowded. To keep a clean and uncluttered appearance, leave all extra information off the nametags and use ribbons to convey it instead.

NECKLACES & LANYARDS

Necklaces and lanyards have become popular nametag holder solutions. Not only do they eliminate the pitfalls of pins or clips, they also offer the added benefit of post-meeting use and exposure.

Necklaces

Although these terms are often used interchangeably, for the sake of discussion, we define necklaces as those hangers that do not accommodate an imprint. Although necklaces don't afford the real estate to sport a sponsor's message, some necklace styles offer an imprint area directly at eye level, just above the nametag, to accommodate a logo or emblem.

As necklaces are not usually customized, they are often kept in stock. Therefore, meeting planners can often order them at the last minute after they have a clear handle on the attendance numbers. In addition, many suppliers will allow a meeting planner to order large quantities in case of a last minute surge in on-site registration and then return the portion that was not used. Alternatively, planners often "stock up" on unused necklaces for future events when they are not company or event-specific. Necklaces are also an excellent choice for those meetings that are not sponsored and, therefore, don't need the added branding space.

Necklaces usually have the disadvantage of coming only in a limited number of colors. This is a consideration when planning your branding efforts. However, they do come in a wide variety of styles. Necklaces are crafted from materials ranging from elastic cord and cloth, to twisted rayon, faux leather and satin, to beads and chains. Necklaces are also offered in either the no-spin or classic configurations.

Lanyards

According to the dictionary, a lanyard is a cord or strap used to hold something, usually worn around the neck. For the meeting planner, a lanyard is basically a necklace made of fabric with the added benefit of offering plenty of space for imprinting a logo, a name or a slogan. Like a necklace, a lanyard again eliminates the need for cumbersome pins or clips.

The higher-quality lanyards make excellent sponsorship items. The extra income earned from selling an excellent advertising opportunity to an organization who wants to get its name in front of a captive, targeted audience can greatly outweigh the extra costs associated.

Their after-meeting use also affords sponsors repeat exposure and therefore an extremely valuable advertising investment. A sponsor's name and/or logo will be constantly reinforced throughout the meeting as attendees wear their nametags to all functions and then will be seen over and over again when the lanyards are taken home.

As key holders

- Easy to find in a crowded purse
- Great for jogging, going to the gym, walking the dog, running errands or whenever purses or pockets are too cumbersome

For employees

- Easy to keep employee IDs, Security Passes or Proxy Cards perpetually accessible
- Helpful for carrying an assortment of work keys around the plant

Flexibility is another advantage of lanyards over necklaces. Lanyards offer many more attachment options and greater latitude to perfectly integrate into the personality of your meeting.

Lanyard quality ranges from the most economical cotton versions to the more substantial nylon or stretchy elastic. Obviously, the larger 1" or 3/4" versions have a larger imprint area to offer your sponsors or for branding potential. The higher quality nylon versions offer a feeling of permanence and are probably more likely to be considered a keepsake, while the less expensive versions still offer a classy option without the added cost. The highest end of the fabric line includes elastic lanyards, which come in a greater color selection.

SELECTING A NECKLACE OR LANYARD

When making your selections, consider your attendees' needs and your branding objectives.

For example, if you're holding an outdoor event, you might want to choose products made of fabric, plastic and rubber instead of metal, which could adversely react with sweat or water. On the other hand, if you are using a necklace or lanyard for a black tie event, you will want to consider metals or finer fabrics. If you're hosting a very casual affair, you might want to consider bigger lanyards in brighter colors.

Next, consider your branding and your artwork. If your logo is very simple, or you just want to add text, most any lanyard will do. However, if your artwork is colorful and complicated, you may want to look for a lanyard or necklace with ample space that affords the room to display it.

For many organizations, their branding is a several million dollar investment that needs to be protected at all costs. If you are creating a meeting for such an event, you will need to be concerned with exact color matching. Most necklaces and lanyard fabrics cannot be matched to an exact PMS color. However, if exact color matching is important to you, consider sublimation. Sublimation allows you to dye the lanyard fabric to your exact specifications. With this process, it's possible to replicate the exact red of the cola giant or precise gold of the famous arches.

Another consideration for your branding is the type of material you choose. The "feel" or the "hand" of a fabric leaves as much of an impression on your attendees as the artwork displayed on it. It all depends on your branding objectives. An elastic cord might be suitable for a conference of non-profit organizations while leather may be more appropriate for your meeting of outdoor sports writers. Consider this: if a shirt was made of this fabric, would you want to wear it? If the answer is no, then don't try to give these to your attendees and expect the results you want.

Lanyard Decorating Options

The highest end offers a woven lanyard in which your logo, message or organization name is actually woven into the product. This is by all means the "Cadillac." This exceptional, top-of-the-line quality demonstrates your commitment to your event, sponsors, staff and to your attendees. Its soft, luxurious feel is complimented by the benefit of two-sided imprinting so your special message will be seen no matter how the fabric falls.

The next lanyard option uses a jacquard braid technique. This technique, developed by Joseph Marie Jacquard in the mid 1800's, offers the benefit of very intricate detail and can reproduce type as small as 8-point. Consider this option for an intricate or multi-colored message on your lanyard.

The final option—the one you'd likely choose if exact color matching is required—would be sublimated or dyed lanyard. While this option is actually less expensive than the previous two, it still exudes quality and can accommodate strict branding requirements. Because each and every order can be dyed to specifications, this option offers nearly perfect color matching with your organization's colors. These lanyards are made of a super soft material and can be imprinted on two sides.

Choosing an attachment for your necklace or lanyard

Finally, you must choose the way you will attach your nametag to your neck piece. This decision might not seem like a very big deal, until you show up at your conference and realize that the choices you made don't work together!

Rubber O-Ring Key Ring J-Hook Bulldog Clip Slim J-Hook

It's important to work with your meeting supplies provider to ensure the choices you are making do, in fact, work together. If you don't know what holder either a sponsor or co-worker is providing, choose a necklace or lanyard that can work with a variety of options. For example, an O-ring with a pin hole can work with a variety of holders and can also accommodate a pin or clip. A split ring with a strap clip can work with either a clip or a slotted holder. Conversely, if you don't know which lanyard attachment will be ordered, choose a holder that works with many options, such as a clip holder with an additional slot.

Bulldog clips and J-hooks are very popular attachment options. They work well with a slotted holder. But, by far, the most popular attachment is the O-ring, which comes in various materials, such as plastic, metal or rubber. It's important to get samples of each prior to making your selection in order to make the best choice to suit your needs.

Another option is the split-ring. These can be recycled to be used as a key ring after your event, elongating the life of a lanyard and its repeat-use possibilities.

Finally, a meeting planner might be concerned with "spin."

In this case, we are talking about the potential of a nametag to turn around showing only a blank backside. Some meeting planners who are concerned about their attendees' ability to effectively network, will choose nametag options that don't allow the badge to turn.

This can be accomplished by using no-spin hooks, which are literally two hooks on each side of the tag, as opposed to one in the center. With the nametag secured at both sides, it's impossible for the attendee's name to ever be hidden. Some meeting planners have come up with another creative solution for the "spin" problem. They simply print two nametags for each attendee and place them back to back in the holder. This way, there's no chance of missing a networking opportunity because the attendees' names are always in view.

There are a few more considerations to make before choosing your attachments. The first is the ease of opening. Meeting planners who wish to have everything organized prior to the attendees' arrivals should consider how difficult the assembly will be.

Opening and attaching thousands of nametags to necklaces or lanyards could be cumbersome if the mechanism is difficult to manipulate. Some planners avoid this problem by giving the attendees the responsibility of their own assembly. Others order samples of various attachments to select the option that will be easiest on themselves or their staff.

Next, think about whether your attendees will be asked to have their badges scanned during the exhibition.

If this will occur, it's a good idea to offer products that will accommodate the situation. There are many products available on the market that will do so. These include the convenient retractable cord addition and the detachable badge for use with electronic scanners. These are exceptionally convenient for trade shows where attendees are asked to scan their card at various booths.

These retractable products can also be used after the meeting as a convenient fastener for employee IDs where security systems require the presentation of a swipeable ID for entry. These allow the wearer to swipe his or her ID without having to look for it and replace it in a pocket or purse.

Variations also include ID clips, belt straps and belt holders. People will certainly appreciate you thinking about the protection of their personal space.

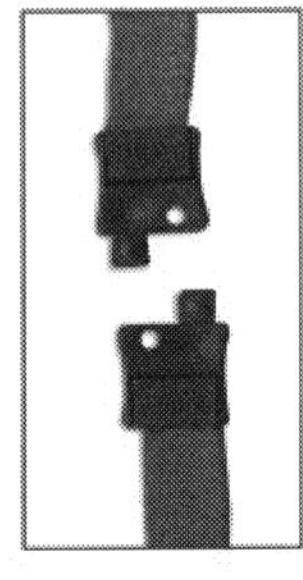

The convenience-release option is also worth consideration. These necklaces "break away" when pulled upon, offering added safety should a necklace get wrapped up with something that could cause strangulation or if attendees are self conscious about mussing up their hair by putting a necklace over their heads.

NAMETAG POUCHES

Pouches offer the convenience of holding a variety of necessities in a wallet or pouch right in the nametag holder. Often times, these impressive solutions actually cost less than purchasing all parts of a nametag system a la carte. Moreover, they are readily sponsor-able as they offer a large imprint area for a sponsor's logo or message.

Pouches allow the attendee to carry a limited amount of cash, credit cards, pens, passports and in some cases, even a palm pilot, notepad or cell phone with them at all times without the risk or burden of carrying a purse or satchel. These types of products are also very popular keepsakes that are used over and over for daily activities. Neck-hung pouches are especially good for keeping belongings safe and accessible while one attends the health club, the beach or during travel.

Be aware, however, that some pouches don't handle ribbons as well as others. If you are planning on using ribbons, make sure you check out samples before you make your purchase.

MEETING REGISTRATION A-L M-Z

RECOGNIZE THEM!

RIBBONS

Nametag ribbons are a great way to recognize, reward and categorize attendees. For a minimal investment, many meeting planners use ribbons to add color and importance to their nametags.

There are two types of ribbons: the traditional tail type and the new, most popular stackable horizontal ribbons.

Tail-type ribbons hang vertically from the nametag. You've seen this type of ribbon before. Think of the State Fair. The problem with these traditional ribbons is that they are sometimes difficult to read as the text usually is run vertically. The other problem is that if someone wears several ribbons they look kind of like the "prize pig" at the fair.

Another option is the newer, horizontal stackable ribbons. Today, this style represents over 75% of ribbons sold as it affords many benefits over the traditional tail type ribbons.

The horizontal ribbon allows for more text, bigger font and is easier to read. It also allows for the stacking of several ribbons for those recipients that are at once a board member, volunteer of the year, gold winner recipient and member for over 30 years. The most popular off-the-shelf titles refer to attendee status, designations and place of residence, such as "Member," "Award Winner," or "Toronto."

Alternatively, some planners like to add fun and levity to their event by using less formal identifiers such as "No Whining" or "Runs With Scissors."

Some organizations have turned this product line into a fun and profitable fund-raiser. They purchase a bundle of stackable ribbons with various sayings and allow attendees to purchase their own identifiers. This is a simple and fun way to raise funds for the organization while giving attendees a chance to express themselves. Even at a buck or two per ribbon, many event planners have raised hundreds of dollars for the good of the organization.

Ribbons have several functions. The first is recognition and reward. Ribbons are a very affordable way to recognize attendees for their myriad contributions to your association or organization. They can also announce to the whole world that this attendee just won a top award in the industry.

The second is categorization. People appreciate being able to easily distinguish various personnel and various attendants. Should someone have a question for staff, it is nice to be able to have them visually identified. Color coding tells an attendee from as far as across the room who's a staff member, who's a speaker, who's an exhibitor, who's an attendee and who is a potential buyer with a large pocketbook.

TIP: When comparing vendors for ribbons, be certain to investigate all hidden costs. Some ribbon manufacturers will offer a seemingly low price for the ribbons, but then tack on an additional charge for the adhesive tape that allows one to apply them to the badges!

CERTIFICATES, AWARDS AND GIFTS

When planning your meeting, be sure to itemize budget lines for certificates, awards and gifts. As these items are intended to impress, congratulate or thank your attendees, you don't want to run out of budget before making these important purchases. Prices in all these categories vary from inexpensive to extravagantly expensive. Again, be certain that you match your choices to your meeting and branding objectives.

CERTIFICATES

Certificates can be used to award the Board of Directors, volunteers, sponsors, donors or attendees for their special accomplishments. This may be through a formal awards contest or as an informal gesture of gratitude. Some meeting planners also provide "Certificates of Completion" for every attendee who completes the education offered at the meeting.

TIP:

To boost the return of your meeting evaluations, consider having your attendees turn in their evaluation to receive their "Certificate of Completion." The meeting planner who created this technique found that the number of evaluations he received skyrocketed from a dismal 20% to over 60%. He waits to print the certificates until after registration, ensuring that any name corrections have already been made. Getting the proper name and spelling on a certificate is critical.

Meeting planners with a large advertising budget and campaign might want to hire a design professional to create their own branded certificates. For those with less budget and time, meeting supply manufacturers offer certificate templates that one can run through a laser printer to personalize with the message, attendee's name and accomplishments. One can enhance the prestige and importance of a certificate with embellishments such as ribbons, gold seals, certificate folders or frames. Your meeting supplier will be able to steer you to various options that are appropriate for your target audience and for your budget.

AWARDS

Many meetings and conferences include an awards ceremony. Awards range from small metal trophies to large crystal and marble statues, costing the meeting planner anywhere from $10 to over $500 on each individual award. Again, when creating your awards budget, keep in mind your audience and the objectives.

There are two basic types of awards, trophy and functional.

Trophy awards are those that would be displayed on a mantle, a shelf in an office or in a case. These are most often given for professional accomplishment, such as the National Addy or the Academy Awards. In this category, it's important to remember that size does matter. The larger the award, the more important it seems.

Material is also important. Unless you can spend $750 plus for a gold plated Oscar, glass and crystal usually carry the highest perceived value.

One of the most popular awards is the tall crystal obelisk. Its imposing shape and beautiful light-catching lines make for a very impressive statement on the recipient's shelf. Nowadays, the purity and clarity of optical glass is so pristine that it can often be mistaken for leaded crystal, saving the meeting planner a lot of money. After glass and crystal, marble exudes the next highest value. However, you always want to check out the quality of the materials used by the manufacturer. Be certain to closely examine samples before ordering.

The other type of award is the functional award. These can be used either as a token of appreciation or as gifts for your speakers, VIPs, board members or volunteers. Again, many functional awards are made of crystal or glass. They are often blown to create bowls, vases, candy dishes, ring holders, drink wear and jewelry boxes.

GIFTS

Meeting planners have many occasions to give gifts to various people involved with a meeting. To be meaningful, the choice of a gift should be considerate of the recipient. What would be useful or impressive to him or her? In addition to the most common key fobs and paperweights, brief cases and watches, there are endless possibilities for gift giving. Be creative. Think outside of the box. And always keep the recipient in mind.

Again, gifts range from relatively inexpensive to outrageously pricey. Be certain to include this line item in your earliest budgets.

RIBBON TITLES

POPULAR

- ❑ #1
- ❑ 5 Years
- ❑ 10 Years
- ❑ 15 Years
- ❑ 20 Years
- ❑ 25 Years
- ❑ 30 Years
- ❑ 40 Years
- ❑ 50 Years
- ❑ First Place
- ❑ Second Place
- ❑ Third Place
- ❑ Fourth Place
- ❑ Fifth Place
- ❑ Sixth Place
- ❑ Academy Member
- ❑ Accredited
- ❑ Active Member
- ❑ Administrative Assistant
- ❑ Admittee
- ❑ Advertiser
- ❑ Advisor
- ❑ Advisor
- ❑ Advisory Board
- ❑ Advisory Committee
- ❑ Advisory Council
- ❑ Affiliate
- ❑ Affiliate Member
- ❑ Alternate
- ❑ Alternate Delegate
- ❑ Alumni
- ❑ Ambassador
- ❑ Analyst
- ❑ Ask Me
- ❑ Assistant
- ❑ Assistant Chair
- ❑ Assistant Chairman
- ❑ Assistant Secretary
- ❑ Assistant Treasurer
- ❑ Associate
- ❑ Associate Member
- ❑ Attendee
- ❑ Audio Visual
- ❑ Author
- ❑ Award
- ❑ Award Nominee
- ❑ Award Recipient
- ❑ Awards Committee
- ❑ Award Winner
- ❑ Benefactor
- ❑ Board
- ❑ Board Alumni
- ❑ Board Executive
- ❑ Board Member
- ❑ Board Of Directors
- ❑ Board Of Governors
- ❑ Board Of Trustees
- ❑ Bronze Sponsor
- ❑ Business Partner
- ❑ Buyer
- ❑ Candidate
- ❑ Captain
- ❑ Certified
- ❑ Certified Instructor
- ❑ CEO
- ❑ Chair
- ❑ Chairman
- ❑ Chairman Of The Board
- ❑ Chairperson
- ❑ Chairwoman
- ❑ Champion
- ❑ Chaplain
- ❑ Chapter Board
- ❑ Chapter Chair
- ❑ Chapter Member
- ❑ Chapter Of The Year
- ❑ Chapter Officer
- ❑ Chapter President
- ❑ Chapter Staff
- ❑ Chapter Vice President
- ❑ Chapter Member
- ❑ CIO
- ❑ Club President
- ❑ CMP
- ❑ Coach
- ❑ Co-Chair
- ❑ Co-Chairman
- ❑ Co-Chairperson
- ❑ Co-Host
- ❑ Commissioner
- ❑ Committee
- ❑ Committee Chair
- ❑ Committee Chairman
- ❑ Committee Chairperson
- ❑ Committee Member
- ❑ Concierge
- ❑ Conference Chair
- ❑ Conference Committee
- ❑ Conference Coordinator
- ❑ Conference Sponsor
- ❑ Conference Staff
- ❑ Consultant
- ❑ Contractor
- ❑ Contributor
- ❑ Convention Chair
- ❑ Convention Chairman
- ❑ Convention Chairperson
- ❑ Convention Committee
- ❑ COO
- ❑ Coordinator
- ❑ Corporate Donor
- ❑ Corporate Member
- ❑ Corporate Sponsor
- ❑ Corporate Supporter
- ❑ Council
- ❑ Council Chair
- ❑ Council Member
- ❑ Customer
- ❑ Dealer
- ❑ Delegate
- ❑ Diamond Sponsor
- ❑ Director
- ❑ Distributor
- ❑ Donor
- ❑ Driver
- ❑ Editor
- ❑ Editorial Board
- ❑ Education
- ❑ Elected Official
- ❑ Emerald Sponsor
- ❑ Emergency Management
- ❑ Emeritus
- ❑ Event Planner
- ❑ Event Sponsor
- ❑ Event Staff
- ❑ Executive Board
- ❑ Executive Committee
- ❑ Executive Council
- ❑ Executive Director
- ❑ Executive Officer
- ❑ Executive Secretary
- ❑ Executive Staff
- ❑ Executive Vice President
- ❑ Exhibit Hall Only
- ❑ Exhibitor
- ❑ Exhibit Staff
- ❑ Expert
- ❑ Expo Manager
- ❑ Facilitator
- ❑ Faculty
- ❑ Fellow
- ❑ Finalist
- ❑ First Timer
- ❑ First Time Attendee
- ❑ First Vice-President
- ❑ Focus Group
- ❑ Foundation
- ❑ Foundation Donor
- ❑ Founder
- ❑ Founding Member
- ❑ Franchisee
- ❑ Friend
- ❑ Gold Sponsor
- ❑ Government
- ❑ Governor
- ❑ Greeter
- ❑ Guest
- ❑ Guest Speaker
- ❑ Guide
- ❑ Hall Of Fame
- ❑ Hello
- ❑ Here To Serve
- ❑ Home Office
- ❑ Honorary Guest
- ❑ Honorary Member
- ❑ Honorable Mention
- ❑ Honored Guest
- ❑ Honoree
- ❑ Hospitality
- ❑ Host
- ❑ Host Chapter
- ❑ Cost Committee
- ❑ Hostess
- ❑ Immediate Past Chairman
- ❑ Immediate Past President
- ❑ Inductee
- ❑ Information
- ❑ Instructor
- ❑ Intern
- ❑ International
- ❑ Interpreter
- ❑ Interviewer
- ❑ Investor
- ❑ Judge
- ❑ Just Promoted
- ❑ Keynote Speaker
- ❑ Leader
- ❑ Leadership Committee
- ❑ Lecturer
- ❑ Legislator
- ❑ Liaison
- ❑ Life Member
- ❑ Local Committee
- ❑ Manager
- ❑ Management
- ❑ Media
- ❑ Mediator
- ❑ Meeting Planner

RIBBON TITLES

- ❑ Member
- ❑ Member At Large
- ❑ Membership Committee
- ❑ Mentor
- ❑ Minister
- ❑ Moderator
- ❑ National Board
- ❑ New Attendee
- ❑ New Exhibitor
- ❑ New Member
- ❑ New Member Associate
- ❑ New Supplier
- ❑ Nominating Committee
- ❑ Nominee
- ❑ Non-Member
- ❑ Nurse
- ❑ Officer
- ❑ Official
- ❑ Official Photographer
- ❑ Official Sponsor
- ❑ Non-Site Personnel
- ❑ Operations
- ❑ Organizer
- ❑ Organizing Committee
- ❑ Owner
- ❑ PAC
- ❑ Panelist
- ❑ Parliamentarian
- ❑ Participant
- ❑ Partner
- ❑ Party Sponsor
- ❑ Past Board Member
- ❑ Past Chair
- ❑ Past President
- ❑ Pastor
- ❑ Patron
- ❑ Planning Committee
- ❑ Platinum Sponsor
- ❑ Plenary Speaker
- ❑ Poster Presenter
- ❑ Premier Sponsor
- ❑ Presenter
- ❑ President
- ❑ President Elect
- ❑ President Emeritus
- ❑ President & CEO
- ❑ President's Club
- ❑ Press
- ❑ Professional Development Committee
- ❑ Program
- ❑ Program Chair
- ❑ Program Chairperson
- ❑ Program Co-Chair
- ❑ Program Committee
- ❑ Perspective Member
- ❑ Protégé
- ❑ Reception
- ❑ Reception Committee
- ❑ Recorder
- ❑ Recreation
- ❑ Registration
- ❑ Registration Committee
- ❑ Regional Director
- ❑ Regional Manager
- ❑ Representative
- ❑ Resident
- ❑ Retailer
- ❑ Retiree
- ❑ Ruby Sponsor
- ❑ Sales Leader
- ❑ Sapphire Sponsor
- ❑ Scholarship Recipient
- ❑ Second Vice-President
- ❑ Secretary
- ❑ Secretary-Treasurer
- ❑ Section Chair
- ❑ Section Chairman
- ❑ Section Chairperson
- ❑ Security
- ❑ Seminar Chairperson
- ❑ Senator
- ❑ Senior Coordinator
- ❑ Senior Vice Chairman
- ❑ Sergeant At Arms
- ❑ Service Management
- ❑ Session Chair
- ❑ Session Chairperson
- ❑ Session Coordinator
- ❑ Session Moderator
- ❑ Session Monitor
- ❑ Show Committee
- ❑ Show Management
- ❑ Show Sponsor
- ❑ Silver Sponsor
- ❑ Speaker
- ❑ Special Guest
- ❑ Sponsor
- ❑ Spouse
- ❑ Staff
- ❑ State Representative
- ❑ Steering Committee
- ❑ Student
- ❑ Student Leader
- ❑ Supervisor
- ❑ Supplier
- ❑ Supporter
- ❑ Sustaining Member
- ❑ Task Force
- ❑ Team Player
- ❑ Treasurer
- ❑ Technology
- ❑ Top Ten
- ❑ Trainee
- ❑ Trainer
- ❑ Trustee
- ❑ Underwriter
- ❑ Usher
- ❑ Vendor
- ❑ Vice Chair
- ❑ Vice Chairman
- ❑ Vice President
- ❑ VIP
- ❑ Visitor
- ❑ Volunteer
- ❑ Voting Delegate
- ❑ Voting Member Welcome
- ❑ Winner

MOTIVATIONAL

- ❑ 110%
- ❑ Attitude
- ❑ Celebrate Diversity
- ❑ Challenge
- ❑ Commitment
- ❑ Community
- ❑ Courage
- ❑ Customer Service
- ❑ Demand Diversity
- ❑ Details
- ❑ Determination
- ❑ Do It Now
- ❑ Educate
- ❑ Ethics
- ❑ Excellence
- ❑ Glory
- ❑ Goals
- ❑ Integrity
- ❑ Leadership
- ❑ New Horizons
- ❑ No Means No
- ❑ Opportunity
- ❑ Pride
- ❑ Quality
- ❑ Recycle
- ❑ Success
- ❑ Teamwork
- ❑ Vision
- ❑ Win

COUNTRIES

- ❑ Argentina
- ❑ Australia
- ❑ Austria
- ❑ Bahrain
- ❑ Belgium
- ❑ Belgique
- ❑ Belize
- ❑ Brazil
- ❑ Brasilia
- ❑ Bulgaria
- ❑ Canada
- ❑ Czech Republic
- ❑ Chile
- ❑ China
- ❑ Colombia
- ❑ Costa Rica
- ❑ Cuba
- ❑ Denmark
- ❑ Danmark
- ❑ Egypt
- ❑ El Salvador
- ❑ England
- ❑ Finland
- ❑ Finlandia
- ❑ France
- ❑ Germany
- ❑ Deutschland
- ❑ Greece
- ❑ Ellas
- ❑ Guatemala
- ❑ Holland
- ❑ Honduras
- ❑ Hong Kong
- ❑ Hungary
- ❑ Iceland
- ❑ India
- ❑ Iran
- ❑ Ireland
- ❑ Eire
- ❑ Israel
- ❑ Italy
- ❑ Italia
- ❑ Japan
- ❑ Nicaragua
- ❑ Nippon
- ❑ Jordan
- ❑ Kenya
- ❑ Korea
- ❑ Mexico
- ❑ Netherlands

RIBBON TITLES

- ❑ New Zealand
- ❑ Norway
- ❑ Pakistan
- ❑ Panama
- ❑ Paraguay
- ❑ Peru
- ❑ Poland
- ❑ Polonia
- ❑ Portugal
- ❑ Portuguesa
- ❑ Russia
- ❑ Saudi Arabia
- ❑ Scotland
- ❑ Singapore
- ❑ South Africa
- ❑ Spain
- ❑ España
- ❑ Sudan
- ❑ Sweden
- ❑ Sverige
- ❑ Switzerland
- ❑ Suisse
- ❑ Syria
- ❑ Taiwan
- ❑ Turkey
- ❑ Uganda
- ❑ Ukraine
- ❑ United Kingdom
- ❑ USA
- ❑ Venezuela
- ❑ Vietnam
- ❑ Wales
- ❑ Yemen
- ❑ Yugoslavia
- ❑ Jugoslavia
- ❑ Zamia

STATES, TERRITORIES & REGIONS

- ❑ Alabama
- ❑ Alaska
- ❑ Arizona
- ❑ Arkansas
- ❑ California
- ❑ Connecticut
- ❑ Delaware
- ❑ Florida
- ❑ Georgia
- ❑ Hawaii
- ❑ Idaho
- ❑ Indiana
- ❑ Illinois
- ❑ Iowa
- ❑ Kansas
- ❑ Kentucky
- ❑ Louisiana
- ❑ Maine
- ❑ Maryland
- ❑ Massachusetts
- ❑ Michigan
- ❑ Minnesota
- ❑ Mississippi
- ❑ Missouri
- ❑ Montana
- ❑ Nebraska
- ❑ Nevada
- ❑ New Hampshire
- ❑ New Jersey
- ❑ New Mexico
- ❑ New York
- ❑ North Carolina
- ❑ North Dakota
- ❑ Ohio
- ❑ Oklahoma
- ❑ Oregon
- ❑ Pennsylvania
- ❑ Rhode Island
- ❑ South Carolina
- ❑ South Dakota
- ❑ Tennessee
- ❑ Texas
- ❑ Utah
- ❑ Vermont
- ❑ Virginia
- ❑ Washington
- ❑ West Virginia
- ❑ Wisconsin
- ❑ Wyoming
- ❑ American Samoa
- ❑ Guam
- ❑ Puerto Rico
- ❑ Virgin Islands
- ❑ Southwest Region
- ❑ Southeast Region
- ❑ Northwest Region
- ❑ West Region
- ❑ East Region
- ❑ North Region
- ❑ South Region
- ❑ Central Region
- ❑ Midwest Region
- ❑ Mid-Atlantic Region
- ❑ Mountain Region

CANADIAN PROVINCES

- ❑ Alberta
- ❑ British Columbia
- ❑ Manitoba
- ❑ New Brunswick
- ❑ Newfoundland
- ❑ Northwest Territories
- ❑ Nova Scotia
- ❑ Nunavut
- ❑ Ontario
- ❑ Prince Edward Island
- ❑ Quebec
- ❑ Saskatchewan
- ❑ Yukon

CITIES

- ❑ Atlanta
- ❑ Boston
- ❑ Chicago
- ❑ Dallas
- ❑ Detroit
- ❑ Houston
- ❑ Los Angeles
- ❑ Miami
- ❑ New York City
- ❑ Orlando
- ❑ Philadelphia
- ❑ St. Louis
- ❑ Toronto
- ❑ Washington, DC

INTERPRETER

- ❑ Atakallam Al'arabiyya (Arabic)
- ❑ Falo Portugues (Portuguese)
- ❑ Parle Français (French)
- ❑ I Speak English (English)
- ❑ Hablo Español (Spanish)
- ❑ Nasema Kiswahili (Swahili)
- ❑ Omilo Ellenika (Greek)
- ❑ I Can Sign
- ❑ Interpreter

FUN ONES

- ❑ All Star
- ❑ Been There, Done That
- ❑ Beginner
- ❑ Big Cheese
- ❑ Bored Member
- ❑ Certifiable
- ❑ Clueless
- ❑ .Com
- ❑ Computer Geek
- ❑ Cool!
- ❑ Coulda Been
- ❑ Diva
- ❑ Egg Head
- ❑ Go Away
- ❑ Goddess
- ❑ Grandma
- ❑ Grandpa
- ❑ Has Been
- ❑ Huh?
- ❑ Insignificant Other
- ❑ Internet Junkie
- ❑ It's A Boy!
- ❑ It's A Girl!
- ❑ It's All About Me
- ❑ Joker
- ❑ Just Married
- ❑ King
- ❑ Know It All
- ❑ Last Place
- ❑ Maxed Out
- ❑ No Whining
- ❑ Nobody
- ❑ Official Something
- ❑ Old Timer
- ❑ Other
- ❑ Party Animal
- ❑ Party Pooper
- ❑ Philosopher
- ❑ Plays Well With Others
- ❑ Prince
- ❑ Princess
- ❑ Queen
- ❑ Queen Bee
- ❑ Rock Star
- ❑ Rookie Of The Year
- ❑ Royalty
- ❑ Runs With Scissors
- ❑ Shepherd
- ❑ $$Show Me The Money$$
- ❑ Somebody
- ❑ Stressed
- ❑ Superstar
- ❑ Sweet!
- ❑ The Answer Is No
- ❑ Tired Feet
- ❑ Trouble Maker
- ❑ Whatever...
- ❑ Workaholic
- ❑ Worker Be
- ❑ Yada Yada Yada

ROUND OUT YOUR BRANDING- SELECTING YOUR MEETING SUPPLIES

Your meeting's branding extends far beyond your logo or even your marketing materials. It encompasses everything you do or say or that you give away. It certainly is impacted by the meeting supplies you choose.

Meeting supplies range from the novelty items planners may send out during the marketing of their meeting, to the registration materials attendees receive in their logo'd tote bag at the registration counter, to the awards of recognition given out at the Gala Ceremony.

Items come in all price categories, from branded giveaway pens to impressive padfolios and leather briefcases.

The sophistication of the meeting supply industry has grown enormously in the last few decades. As the industry has advanced, more refined research and information has been made available. Meeting supply manufacturers study trends, needs and the success of each of their products to be able to guide planners to the very best solutions available.

For the meeting planner, meeting supply companies offer headache-saving solutions that will allow you to focus on the myriad of other details before you. Rely on this expertise. Most are more than willing to work with you through all the details to develop an appropriate mix of supplies to meet your function's needs and budget.

It is important to take into consideration the supplies you will need when you are designing the initial budget. You don't want to get caught short at the last minute!

REGISTRATION MATERIALS

Remember, the registration experience is the first on-site impression your attendees will have of your meeting. This impression can greatly affect how the rest of the meeting is perceived. So, it's critical that is a good impression!

In addition to being well staffed and organized, it is important to present registration materials in neat, well-branded packaging. At the registration counter, you will have the opportunity to "wow" your attendees with high-quality, personalized attention to detail or disappoint them with a shoddy, disorganized, unimpressive welcome that conveys you don't really care much about them. Visualize what you would like to receive if you were attending your meeting and plan backward from there.

Registration materials can be considered anything that the attendee receives at the registration counter. You will need to accommodate: nametags, necklaces, ribbons, agendas, maps, location advice, hotel data and any other information you'd like to share about your meeting or the sponsoring company. Attendees feel appreciated when you help them make their stay more comfortable and enjoyable without having to figure out the lay of the land themselves.

It is also nice to give your attendees branded equipment that will help them get the most out of the meeting and that they can take home as a useable souvenir. Valuable giveaways can include anything from calculators to pens to water bottles and pouches.

Of course, all of these will need to be packaged in a convenient and attractive manner. If your budget doesn't allow for briefcases or totes, meeting suppliers offer customized registration envelopes that totally integrate into the branding and color scheme of your meeting.

Meeting supply companies also offer filing and organization systems that will help keep the registration process seamlessly flowing. The last thing a meeting planner wants to do is look disorganized, or make an attendee wait while he/she hunts for his/her registration materials. (See Chapter 3 for more information about planning for registration materials).

TAKE NOTE! *ATTENDEES APPRECIATE WRITING ESSENTIALS*

It's often a valued gesture to supply your attendees with writing essentials to use during your meeting. This is also a great branding opportunity as pens, paper and padfolios almost always make it into the suitcase for use back home.

PENS, PENCILS AND OTHER WRITING INSTRUMENTS

You'd be surprised how many attendees are already searching for a pen or pencil at the registration counter! Giving away branded writing instruments is a very effective way to get your message in front of everyone. Pens are rarely thrown away and almost guarantee repeat exposure. Moreover, you'll look like a hero to the attendee who can't seem to find his.

The writing instruments category offers you many options and choices. Before you make your selections, first review your branding thesis, your meeting's objectives and your target audience. Then, with this compass in hand, choose the products that most closely point in its direction.

A meeting planner can spend as little as a quarter or as much a hundred dollars-plus per unit on a pen or pencil giveaway. In addition to putting a less expensive pen in each registration package, meeting planners often scatter holders of pens around the registration table and in meeting rooms for attendees' convenience and added branding exposure. High-end pens, pencils and sets are usually reserved for gifts presented in fancy boxes. In the middle of the spectrum, there are numerous choices at dozens of price points to allow you to make the impression you desire.

There are many, many possibilities to consider when electing your writing tool giveaway and the coordinating investment. You'll have to make choices concerning the type, the tip, the body, the clip, the finish, the colors and the capacity for branding.

And you thought this was going to be simple!

THE TOOL TYPE

You'll first want to consider which writing tool will best meet your objectives.

Basic lead pencils are the most economical option in this category. While pencils do offer limited opportunity for branding or adding your message, their popularity has dropped substantially in the last several years. Mechanical pencils are a step up from the basic model and are available with multiple options in various price ranges. Meeting planners might choose this tool for specialized groups, such as accountants or architects, who use pencils on a daily basis.

In the pen category, there are even more varieties to choose from.

The most economical is the stick pen. This is the basic cylindrical pen with no frills or enhancements.

An upgraded version is the retractable option. Of course, a retractable pen is slightly more costly than a stick. However, it eliminates the problem of losing a cap or potentially staining a pocket or purse and lends a greater perceived value. Retractable pens come in either a twist or click variety.

Combination writing tools—the next price category—are a relatively new innovation in the industry.

Because of their unique nature and supreme convenience, combination tools can be used to really impress attendees. Many meeting planners find that guests appreciate the highlighter/ball point or highlighter/felt tip combinations as they make it easy to switch back and forth between taking notes and accenting salient points on handouts.

Another new innovation is the combination pen/flashlight that allows attendees to take notes during presentations in a darkened room. With so many speakers now using electronic presentations, this product has become extremely popular.

You will find a myriad of combo products—from key chain/pens to pens with four different colored inks to suit any meeting or audience.

THE TIP

These days, you have more freedom of choice than simply the traditional pencil and a ball point. You now have the additional options of fountain pens, felt tips, roller ink, gel ink and highlighters in a whole rainbow of colors.

As with everything, you'll need to be aware of trends—even in the world of pens and ink. Today, in addition to the traditional colors of black, blue and red, translucent and pastel ink colors are also available. When making your selection, again consider your audience. Translucent hot pink ink might not go over as well for your National Convention for CPAs as it could be for the Annual Conference of Scrap-booking Aficionados.

THE BODY

It seems like there once was a day when all pens came in a traditional body that was a slim 1/4" in diameter and approximately 5 1/2" long. That's no longer the case. Recent ergonomic advances have produced the wide body pen and the comfort grip feature, both of which promise to reduce the amount of hand fatigue when taking notes.

Today's suppliers also offer non-traditional alternatives.

The compact pen is a mini version which allows one to keep a pen even in the smallest compartment. The three-sided pen affords the meeting planner triple the number of advertising surfaces. And the novelty shaped pen can be fashioned into a logo or a symbol of the industry, such as a plane, a heart or a star.

THE FINISH

Pen finishes range from the most economical to the most extravagant. The most affordable pens are made of plastic and the most expensive are 24K gold plated. In between, you will find lacquer, wood, chrome, nickel plate, chrome plate and palladium plate, as well as various combinations thereof.

THE CLIP

Even clips come in options, from the most traditional to the most contemporary designs and are now available in break-resistant varieties.

THE BRANDING

When making your selection, be certain to consider each option's capacity for branding. The most economical stick and retractable varieties often come with your choice of both barrel and trim colors, allowing you to coordinate your pens with your meeting's color scheme. Next, consider the imprinting options each pen makes available. Some pens accommodate screen printing, others offer laser engraving and some offer a choice of both. Then consider the size of the available imprint space. Some pens can accommodate a graphic or logo, others will only allow for a text message. Some offer the ability to use multiple imprints and others offer space to advertise on both the pen's barrel and clip. Finally consider the imprint color options. Various pens will accommodate from one to four imprint colors.

It's always a good idea to order samples of the pens you are considering. This way, you can see the actual size of the imprint area and can test the writing quality. A pen that writes unevenly or roughly will render the impression of low quality and will most likely be tossed away, leaving a poor reflection on you.

WRITING PADS

Another essential tool is the writing pad. These pads of paper are easy to imprint with your meeting's name and tagline or the logo and slogan of your sponsor. Again, you'd likely be doing your attendees a favor by providing them with what they need to take notes. Of course, these note pads will go home with them and will provide repeat exposure until the pads are used up. Then, they might be filed away, along with the attendees' notes, again reinforcing your branding when they're pulled out to be reviewed in months and years to come.

Providing logo'd paper pads is a relatively inexpensive way to enhance both your branding and your attendees' satisfaction. Nearly any printer offers pad printing. Your design, message or logo is printed onto the sheets and then glued together to form pads. The most common pad sizes are the traditional 8 1/2" x 11" letter size and the half sized, 8 1/2" x 5 1/2", although you can create pads in nearly any size and shape you desire. Consider the type of meeting and what your audience would most likely prefer. Many people like the traditional letter size as it gives them plenty of area to write notes and fits much better into the file upon getting back to the office.

You also have a myriad of design options to play with. You can stamp your logo at the top of a legal pad, print your meeting name and motto at the top of a blank page or screen back your graphic over the entire work surface so that notes are taken right over it. Work with your designer and printer to create the best option for your meeting.

PADFOLIOS

For those meeting planners with the budget, or the sponsorship to support it, a padfolio is an excellent giveaway for a meeting. Not only does it answer the attendees' immediate needs with an organized way to keep their notes and belongings, it also is most often an item that will receive repeated use. In addition, it can be a classy device to hold and deliver registration materials.

Padfolios are a way to encase a writing pad and will often accommodate other important items to have on hand during the meeting—or later at home—during a professional's business day.

The most economical padfolios are vinyl, usually screen printed with the meeting branding and slogan on the front, and offer no extra pockets or closure.

The upgraded versions usually come with various pockets and some sort of closure device. Meeting supplies experts have found that people like to be able to zip up their belongings and their work so that nothing falls out or flips open for all the world to see.

These padfolios, like all meeting supplies, are available in various price categories depending on the material they're made from, the number and type of organizational compartments, the quality of closure and the decoration method chosen.

You can chose from the most affordable leather-like vinyl, durable and sporty canvas, faux leather or the recently invented, and very popular, microfiber. Of course, if you have to make an extremely good impression, you can always opt for genuine leather. However, leather is very expensive. You'll have to weigh the return on investment for spending so much on a personal item that may or may not be as appreciated as much as you would like.

When choosing a padfolio, consider the options each offers for organization. Most will offer a slot to hold a pen, which, of course, is an imperative. In addition, many will also offer compartments to hold business cards, credit cards, discs and handouts. Some versions even offer a zippered compartment to hold extra supplies and valuables.

There are many options for decorating your padfolios. Work with your supplier to choose the one that makes the most sense for you. The most simple is a screenprinting in one to several colors. The others are embossing, debossing and foil stamping. Embroidery tends to lend the highest perceived value, making your giveaway more likely to be used again. However, remember to plan ahead, because embroidery is usually more expensive and takes more lead time.

When decorating a padfolio or other product you hope the recipients will reuse, remember that less can be more. A quality padfolio with an elegantly embroidered mark or subtle embossed logo is much more likely to be reused than one with a huge garish logo imprinted on it which screams "I got this freebie at a conference!"

BAGS AND TOTES

These days, it's almost become expected to receive a tote bag when attending a meeting. Bags can carry the meeting's branding and can easily be sponsored. They are very convenient for attendees to tote their registration materials from room to room and are essential for meetings with trade shows where exhibitors notoriously hand out samples, specialty items and company literature.

When selecting your bag or tote, be certain to consider both size and quality.

The size of the bag you choose should be appropriate to the type of meeting you are having and the quantity of materials you'll be handing out. Too large a bag with nearly nothing in it will appear as silly as giving out adorable, but petite, bags to haul out onto the trade show floor.

Because of the nature of photography, a representation in a catalog can't always give you an accurate idea of the size and feel of an item. If at all possible, try to test out various sized bags with the amount of registration materials you anticipate you'll be providing. Nearly all suppliers are happy to send out samples.

Next, consider the quality of the bag and the image you want to project. As Melissa Anunson, Meeting Supplies Specialist, says, "You can choose the best of the worst or the worst of the best." In bags and totes, nothing could be more true. Higher-end paper bags might make a more elegant statement than the lowest end of the more expensive fabric bag category. It all depends on your meeting's branding, its audience and the amount of repeat exposure you desire.

PAPER AND PLASTIC

The economy end of the bag and tote spectrum offers bags made of paper or plastic. The least expensive options include either the simple kraft paper or the basic plastic bag. Both of these options are available in various sizes, can accommodate a simple imprint and are usually available for rush orders.

When selecting these options, know that while you are providing a convenience for your attendees that will reinforce your branding, these choices will likely be "left for the maid" when packing up for home. Depending on your budget and your branding objectives, this may be totally appropriate. Just be aware of the limited exposure potential for these options.

A slight enhancement to both the price and the exposure potential is the zippered plastic bag which, much like newer household plastic bags, offers a zip-close option. This simple extra feature will likely increase repeat exposure as it becomes an excellent storage for wet or dirty clothes and is likely to make its way into the luggage.

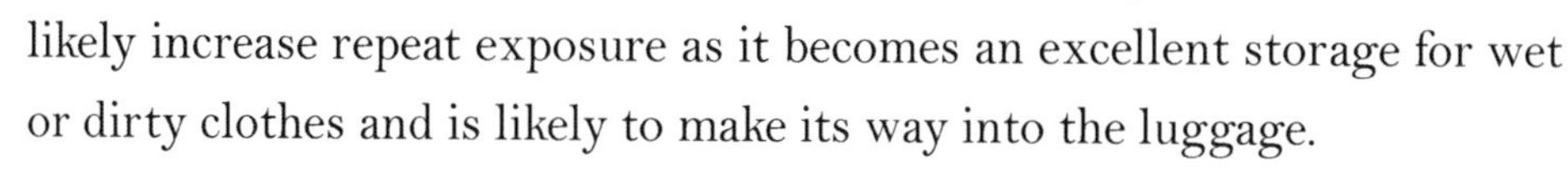

The more impressive, luxury options in this category include rope-handled color imprinted bags like the ones you'd find at a high-end retail store or the upscale frosted translucent bags. These bags are much more durable and offer the option to use foil imprints, which instantly create a refined and polished impression.

Just as most people save the high-quality bags they receive at Sax Fifth Avenue or Gucci, the luxury-end paper meeting bags are almost sure to end up going onto the plane or into the suitcase for use back home.

Tissue paper, especially metallics, can be used to add even more drama and value to a bag filled with giveaways or registration materials. It's just this type of attention to detail that can add class and distinction to any meeting-even those on the tightest of budgets.

The pocket bag is a recent addition to the totes line and will certainly demonstrate your attention to your attendees' needs. These bags offer a pocket to place a duplicate of the attendee's nametag, so on the busy trade show or cafeteria floor, it will be easy to figure out which bag belongs to whom. Your attendees will certainly be impressed when they arrive at your registration counter to receive their materials in a bag personalized with their name right on the front.

FABRIC

The next level of bags and totes jumps to fabric bags. Typically, the use of fabric automatically pushes an item from the disposable to the "must keep" column. Fabric bags also offer the advantage of longer, over-the- shoulder handles, which are not yet available for paper or most plastic bags.

Fabric quality ranges from the most disposable polypropylene to the most savable heavy-duty canvas to the cream of the crop, leather.

The fabric economy option is polypropylene. It's durable, comes in assorted colors and is able to grab and display vibrant ink colors. As many people liken this material to that used on airline pillows, it does not exude the same high quality as other fabrics.

The next fabric quality level is cotton sheeting. This is a muslin-like fabric that starts in a natural color and can be bleached or dyed into a wide variety of colors. Cotton sheeting makes for an affordable, yet attractive, bag or tote.

Canvas is the next step higher in quality. Canvas has greater durability and a heavier feel than cotton sheeting. It projects a classic, sporty image. Canvas is a heavy-weight, rough weave cotton material that's used for anything from tennis shoes to oil paintings to, of course, bags and totes. It is measured in "duck weight" with the highest number, ironically, designating the lightest material. For example, a #4 duck weight canvas is considered extra heavy weight, whereas a #12 is considered light weight. Products made of light-colored canvas are the best options for heattransfer or reproducing 4-color photography. Either white or natural work well.

Polyester and nylon are used to create the popular higher-end bags and totes. These materials are measured in Denier. The definition of "Denier" is a measure of fiber fineness. It's used to measure the quality of silk and some artificial fibers, such as polyester and nylon. Denier is a direct numbering system in which the lower numbers represent the finer sizes and the higher numbers the coarser sizes. For example a 450 denier yarn is twice as fine as 900 denier yarn. The higher the Denier in a particular material the higher the strength and weight of the fabric. This measurement gives the meeting planner some idea of the quality of a product she sees in a catalog or on a Web site, but can be confusing as each type of material is different. For example, a 420D nylon bag will be stronger than a 600D polyester one. As with all specialty items, it's a good idea to request a sample to truly gauge how the bag will look and feel.

Again, of course, the Cadillac of all tote materials is leather, but in most cases, its high price makes it impractical for many meeting planners' needs.

KICK IT UP A NOTCH!

The highest level of totes includes back packs and briefcases. These have been designed to accommodate the professional's everyday business needs with multiple, specialized pockets and compartments. In addition, they've been crafted from high quality materials that will hold up for years of daily use. Back packs and briefcases are a little pricier than other totes, but make a powerful and lasting impression. They're often used to reward VIPs, board members, speakers or attendees of an exclusive meeting.

THE REST OF THE STORY

OK. You thought you now knew everything there is about bags and totes. Guess again. When making your selection, here are a few more issues to consider.

Get a Handle on It

As the majority of people like being able to throw a bag - especially a heavy one - over their shoulders, instead of carrying them, look for handles that are at least 23 inches in length. For added comfort, some bags come with padded handles or the option of either a shoulder or carry handle.

To Gusset or Not to Gusset

The dictionary defines a gusset as "inset piece of fabric, usually triangular in shape, inserted in a garment where added strength or freedom of movement is needed." In the world of meeting bags, gussets add the flat bottom that allows a bag to sit on its own on a table or the floor. Less expensive bags do not have gussets and are shaped more like envelopes that are not able to stand up on their own.

You Can Never Have Too Many Pockets

The most economical totes offer a single space for storage, while those at the higher end offer multiple and zippered compartments. The highest end bags now even offer specially designed pockets for today's professional necessities such as laptops, computer discs, calculators, water bottles, cell phones and pagers.

For that personal touch and convenience, some bags and briefcases also offer a compartment to showcase a duplicate nametag or business card.

THE ICING ON THE CAKE

Here's where the fun comes in, decorating and branding your bag. The possibilities are endless!

Again, remember the image you are trying to convey and start from there. You can mark your bag with your meeting theme, organization's logo or a special message you want attendees to take back with them. This can be done boldly or subtly in one to full-color imprinting or the most impressive branding option, embroidery. Embroidery automatically adds value to an item. The texture and vivid color pops your logo off the background and its high quality causes the recipient to know, "Hey, they like me. They really, really like me!"

Remember, the higher quality the product, the more likely it will have repeat exposure for your meeting or your sponsor.

Luxurious retail-type bags get saved and reused all the time. A canvas bag will almost certainly be recycled into a tote to carry things to the office, school or hobby sessions. And, a sponsor or meeting marketer can feel pretty confident that no one will throw away a high-end back pack or briefcase. Even if the 9-year-old inherits the backpack to use for school, just think of the number of people that will see your organization's or your sponsor's logo day after day!

MEETING SUPPLY TIMETABLE

Plan Ahead When Ordering Meeting Supplies

When backing out the timetable before your meeting, be sure you not only allow enough time for production of supplies, but also enough time for the other parts of the process: reviewing samples, approving quotations and artwork proofs, shipping (to your office and/or to your meeting site), and assembly.

3-6 MONTHS BEFORE YOUR MEETING:

- ❑ Create a wish list of meeting supplies that will enhance your meeting's brand and attendee experience. Consider the type of meeting you're planning and which items—from totes, padfolios and pens to gift giveaways like calculators and PDAs would best compliment your meeting and its sponsor.
- ❑ Approach potential sponsors to underwrite these costs.

8 WEEKS BEFORE YOUR MEETING:

- ❑ Review samples of the vast array of lanyard options available. Some have long production times, so you'll want to make sure you have ample time to produce the lanyard of your choice.
- ❑ Many types of awards also have fairly long production times.

6 WEEKS BEFORE YOUR MEETING:

- ❑ Get samples and start an order of custom badge holders.

4-5 WEEKS BEFORE YOUR MEETING:

- ❑ Bring in samples of bags or totes for review. You'll want to order these at least 3 weeks ahead of your meeting.

3 WEEKS BEFORE YOUR MEETING:

- ❑ Order custom badge stock and custom ribbons. Add additional time for printing and assembly if you'll need it.

1 WEEK BEFORE YOUR MEETING:

- ❑ Order any last-minute items. Most suppliers offer a rush service in case you have a surge in registration and need extra product really fast—you can usually have it the next day.

PACKING UP TO GO

Getting packed and ready for an out-of-town conference can produce anxiety for any meeting planner. You have to visualize being on site and anticipate all the possible things you will need.

When you're on site, you will basically be running a make-shift office. So start from there. What are all the supplies you'll need to run your office and event? Then organize all your materials so that you'll be able to access your materials in the order that you'll need them.

> *TIP: When packing for your registration, consider using inexpensive cardboard boxes for items that will only travel one way and more durable plastic distribution totes for those that will come back with you.*

Number your boxes as you go along and prepare a packing list that describes the contents of each of the numbered boxes. This is extremely important. Not only will it help you remember everything as you're packing, but it will be critical on site. Distribute a copy of this list to all staff members that are going to the meeting.

The first person to arrive at the hotel should be instructed to immediately take the list and go to the luggage room to check if all boxes are present and accounted for. The numbering system makes it easy to check. Should a box or two be missing, the packing list will quickly show exactly what's not there without having to open up each and every box. Then, depending on what was in those boxes, the employee can make arrangements to replace the supplies either locally or by having someone back at the office re-send whatever's needed.

ACME ASSOCIATION MEETING
Box #1 — Registration Materials
Box #2 — Registration Packages
Box #3 — Computer Equipment
Box #4 — Electrical
Box #5 — Business Set
Box #6 — Office Supplies
Box #7 — Accounting Supplies
Box #8 — Communication
Box #9 — Registration Area
Box #10 — Emergency Container

REGISTRATION PACKAGES

The first set of boxes will contain everything that goes into the registration packages, such as name badges, ribbons, programs, registration forms and tickets, if applicable. You might also bring along materials from the meeting city's Convention & Visitors Bureau or from your organization. If you're adding specialty items, such as pens or padfolios, you'll want to pack those with the other things that will need to be assembled into the registration packages. And, of course, you don't want to forget your registration envelopes or totes. For on-site organization and efficiency, you might bring along pre-printed labels or badges to easily identify each attendee's package.

REGISTRATION MATERIALS

- ❑ On-site registration forms
- ❑ Copies of brochures
- ❑ Programs
- ❑ Evaluations
- ❑ Certificates
- ❑ Awards

REGISTRATION PACKAGE MATERIALS

- ❑ Name badges
- ❑ Ribbons
- ❑ Programs
- ❑ Promotional materials
- ❑ City-specific materials
- ❑ Specialty items
- ❑ Registration packages or totes

New organization devices are now available to better manage your registration materials. Nametag cases and organizers allow the meeting planner to set up nametags prior to leaving for the event, transport them safely and save precious room on the registration counter.

These come in various materials from PVC to hard nylon to wood.

In addition, there are ribbon organizers that keep ribbons categorized and ready to use from meeting to meeting.

ON-SITE OFFICE

The next set of boxes will contain all that you'll need to set up your office: files, computer equipment and accessories, office supplies, communication devices and stationery.

Many meeting suppliers now offer many airline-conformant luggage options that not only ensure the safe arrival of materials, but also provide easy on-site organization and storage.

COMPUTER EQUIPMENT

- ❑ Computers
- ❑ Printers
- ❑ Cables
- ❑ Back-up disks
- ❑ Back-up printers & computers
- ❑ Toner

ELECTRICAL

- ❑ Power strips
- ❑ Extension cords

BUSINESS SET

- ❑ Stationery
- ❑ Letterhead
- ❑ Envelopes

OFFICE SUPPLIES

- ❑ Paper
- ❑ File boxes
- ❑ Pens, pencils & markers
- ❑ Staplers & staples
- ❑ Tape
- ❑ Pads of paper
- ❑ Packing tape
- ❑ Paper clips
- ❑ Scissors
- ❑ Rubber bands

ACCOUNTING SUPPLIES

- ❑ Cash
- ❑ Cash boxes
- ❑ Credit card slips
- ❑ Credit card machines
- ❑ Deposit slips
- ❑ Deposit stamp
- ❑ Deposit book
- ❑ Deposit envelopes
- ❑ Calculator
- ❑ Date & number stampers

COMMUNICATION

- ❑ Walkie talkies
- ❑ Hotel phone list
- ❑ Staff cell phone list

Higher-end options allow you to "take your office with you" by offering you shipping cases that keep all of your papers and office supplies, such as extra badges, staplers, paper clips and shipping tape, secure and organized. Once you get on site, there's no unpacking. Simply unlock the case and you're all set for business. Especially for meeting planners that are on the road several times a year, this can be a very affordable lifesaver.

There are also various flight cases available that safely transport computers, printers and projectors. These cases are padded with high-density foam to protect your valuable electronics and are encased in an ultra durable material to withstand all the rigors of air travel.

REGISTRATION AREA

The next set of boxes will contain the all-important items for your registration area. These might include: vases, directional signage, easels, ballot boxes, roll tickets, convention candy and drink tokens.

REGISTRATION AREA MATERIALS

- ❑ Vases
- ❑ Directional signage
- ❑ Easels
- ❑ Ballot boxes
- ❑ Roll tickets
- ❑ Convention candy
- ❑ Drink tokens

EMERGENCY KIT

As a meeting planner, you can never be too prepared. You never know when your meeting will find itself inside a hurricane, a tornado or a debilitating blizzard.

EMERGENCY CONTAINER

- ❑ Tool kit
- ❑ First aid kit
- ❑ Aspirin
- ❑ Polaroid
- ❑ Digital camera
- ❑ Lost badge forms
- ❑ Incident reports
- ❑ Accident forms
- ❑ Megaphone
- ❑ Pens
- ❑ Pads
- ❑ Rain ponchos
- ❑ Resuscitator
- ❑ Personnel roster
- ❑ Emergency phone numbers
- ❑ Extra batteries & flashlights
- ❑ Weather radio
- ❑ Radio
- ❑ Water

One meeting planner uses a red plastic tote to carry all of the emergency equipment and first aid to each of his meetings. He keeps the tote packed with extra water, batteries, flashlights, aspirin and anything he can think of to be ready for an emergency. Everyone knows where the red tote is and what's in it.

Travel-ready utility carts are a relatively new offering for meeting planners. These carts break down for easy travel and then snap together in a minute to carry your supplies and AV equipment into the hotel and from your room to the registration table and then to the various meeting facilities.

PACKING CHECKLIST

ORGANIZATION
- ❑ Packing list in all briefcases
- ❑ Shipping tracking numbers

REGISTRATION MATERIALS
- ❑ On-site registration forms
- ❑ Copies of brochures
- ❑ Programs
- ❑ Evaluations
- ❑ Certificates
- ❑ Awards

REGISTRATION PACKAGE MATERIALS
- ❑ Name badges
- ❑ Ribbons
- ❑ Programs
- ❑ Promotional materials
- ❑ City-specific materials
- ❑ Specialty items
- ❑ Registration packages or totes

COMPUTER EQUIPMENT
- ❑ Computers
- ❑ Printers
- ❑ Cables
- ❑ Back-up disks
- ❑ Back-up printers & computers
- ❑ Toner

ELECTRICAL
- ❑ Power strips
- ❑ Extension cords

BUSINESS SET
- ❑ Stationery
- ❑ Letterhead
- ❑ Envelopes

OFFICE SUPPLIES
- ❑ Paper
- ❑ File boxes
- ❑ Pens, pencils & markers
- ❑ Staplers & staples
- ❑ Tape
- ❑ Pads of paper
- ❑ Packing tape
- ❑ Paper clips
- ❑ Scissors
- ❑ Rubber bands

ACCOUNTING SUPPLIES
- ❑ Cash
- ❑ Cash boxes
- ❑ Credit card slips
- ❑ Credit card machines
- ❑ Deposit slips
- ❑ Deposit stamp
- ❑ Deposit book
- ❑ Deposit envelopes
- ❑ Calculator
- ❑ Date & number stampers

COMMUNICATION
- ❑ Walkie talkies
- ❑ Hotel phone list
- ❑ Staff cell phone list

REGISTRATION AREA MATERIALS
- ❑ Vases
- ❑ Directional signage
- ❑ Easels
- ❑ Ballot boxes
- ❑ Roll tickets
- ❑ Convention candy
- ❑ Drink tokens

EMERGENCY CONTAINER
- ❑ Tool kit
- ❑ First aid kit
- ❑ Aspirin
- ❑ Polaroid
- ❑ Digital camera
- ❑ Lost badge forms
- ❑ Incident reports
- ❑ Accident forms
- ❑ Megaphone
- ❑ Pens
- ❑ Pads
- ❑ Rain ponchos
- ❑ Resuscitator
- ❑ Personnel roster
- ❑ Emergency phone numbers
- ❑ Extra batteries & flashlights
- ❑ Weather radio
- ❑ Radio
- ❑ Water

STAFFING UP

Another thing you'll need to consider well before packing up are your on-site staffing needs.

HOW MANY PEOPLE WILL YOU NEED?

Maximizing your staffing needs is a critical call for the meeting manager. If you don't have enough trained staff present during certain hours, you're going to frustrate attendees, increase the risk of mistakes and reduce your chance of making a good first impression. On the other hand, if you're over-staffed, you're throwing profits out the window. Typically, you'll need a full crew for set up and the first day of registration and can get by with a skeletal staff from the second day on. As a reference, you probably can plan on letting 75% of your staff go after the first day of registration.

You'll also want to determine the ratio of the number of your own employees to local, temporary help.

If the majority of your anticipated attendance has pre-registered, you can get by with a smaller overall staff and more local help. However, if you're expecting a lot of on-site registrations or money exchange, you might want to bring more of your own employees. You probably don't want to trust either money handling or important accounting procedures to temporary or volunteer workers.

MONEY MATTERS

In fact, if at all feasible, you will also want to consider bringing along one of your accounting staff to be in charge of all money matters. During the pandemonium that usually accompanies a meeting, solid, strict accounting practices often go right out the window.

Picture this. A meeting planner hasn't had more than four hours of sleep for the last three nights. Everyone wants something from her and she can't finish even one thing without someone else calling after her. At some point, an attendee shows up at the registration counter demanding his refund. He claims that earlier this morning the meeting planner waived his fee due to a family emergency. Tired and frazzled, she has no recollection of the conversation nor has any records. What is she to do? Had she brought along someone dedicated to managing the accounting, she wouldn't have found herself in this situation.

It's also important to make sure you have enough staff and the proper processes in place to ensure credit card approval on site. Without these, you could end up back at the office with a denied card and no leverage to collect the funds.

LOCAL TALENT

In addition, you might want to round out your on-site personnel with local talent. There are several sources for on-site temporary help. First, you might be lucky enough to recruit volunteer or inexpensive help from either the chamber of commerce or the local chapter of the association sponsoring the meeting. Another option is the hotel. Sometimes hotel staff is interested in picking up extra work. These people obviously know the layout of the hotel and are accustomed to working with customers in a meeting setting. Work with your hotel contact for referrals.

Temporary agencies are another option for staffing. There are even agencies that specialize in providing staff for meetings and registration. Employees from these agencies bring the advantage of understanding meeting processes and are often proficient in various meeting software packages.

DIVERSITY IS IMPORTANT

No matter from where you recruit your staff, remember the importance of diversity. Try to hire a team that mirrors the make up of your audience. When your attendees are in a strange city and walk up to your registration counter, it's much more comfortable to be greeted by a staff that feels familiar. If your meeting will be attracting an international audience, compose a staff that is also international in background.

MANAGING YOUR ON-SITE STAFF

To be able to give your attendees the absolute best first impression of your meeting, you'll want to make sure staff is as knowledgeable and as prepared as possible before the registration counter opens.

COMBINE TRAINING WITH ASSEMBLY

Here's a way to save money and to kill two birds with one stone. You might consider hiring all staff members to come in the day before registration opens for training and for registration package assembly. This way, everyone is familiar with what's in the packet. Then walk everyone through the materials so they know more about the organization and what type of information is available. You might also consider taking a walk through the hotel so that the personnel will be able to direct attendees to the first session and to other important things, such as the rest rooms, phone banks and concierge.

During this session, it's wise for the astute meeting planner to be very observant. Watch the staff and you'll see who are the hardest workers, who's on the ball or who talks too much. Then, you can assign tasks and set up staffing accordingly.

CLEARLY DEFINE EXPECTATIONS OF YOUR STAFF

Seasoned meeting planners might not remember what it was like to go on their first business trip out of town. It probably was very exciting, maybe even a little scary. And likely, you weren't sure what to expect. A good meeting planner will take the time to communicate expectations clearly, without being condescending or overbearing.

First, you want to make sure you are accounting for overtime. During a meeting setting, it's pretty easy to ramp up ten to fourteen hour days. However, if you're bringing along non-exempt employees, you'll want to remember that they usually must be paid time-and-a-half for over time. If you're not mindful, you could end up with "Budget Buster" time cards when you return to the office.

Be certain to review your company's overtime policy and set up on-site procedures that are within legal bounds. In advance, agree what hours they'll be paid for, which events you expect them to attend and work, and which events are optional and unpaid. For example, you might make attendance of the Gala Dinner available to your staff as a perk. If you're clear with them that this is unpaid, totally optional and their presence is not required, they have a choice of how to spend their free time. This up front communication often solves any potential problems.

On the other hand, create a system that affords you some flexibility. If one of your volunteers calls in sick, leaving you short-handed, you want a way to offer employees overtime when they step in and help out with registration. You might simply state that no overtime will be honored without prior authorization.

In addition, you'll want to clearly outline your expectations of your employees on site. You might want to allocate some free time to staffers and explain to them that this is "their time" to go and explore the sites. However, at all other times, they're expected to be on time, refreshed, professional and an ambassador of the meeting. When they're on, they're expected to "be on."

Most meeting planners find that a clearly firm, but generous, schedule works best for all involved. After all, the first time to New Orleans might be very seductive to the new employee who's never been out of state. But realistically, one cannot enjoy beignets and chicory coffee until 3AM and then show up bright eyed at the registration table at 7AM.

Tell 'em who's boss.

Designate one person to be in charge whenever you're not in the immediate vicinity. This person should be the "go to person" should any attendee require special help or need a decision made. This should be someone who is aware of your organization's customer service policies and has the authority to make on-the-spot decisions. Everyone should know to direct any thing that's not routine to this person if the meeting planner is not immediately available.

Take a tip from Sam, greet 'em at the door.

You might also want to assign some of your personnel to be greeters. Greeters are the first people that the attendee will see. The greeter's job, outside of the obvious welcoming, is to double check registration information and to point people to the most appropriate line for them. You don't want people requiring a lot of attention to get into the same line as those that just need to pick up their badges. If you double check the registration information, you can make quick changes on site so that you have all the correct information should there be an emergency or for planning next year's meeting.

Greeters can also be used to work with disabled or elderly attendees. Have your greeters take those with special needs aside to tell them what arrangements you've made for them and find out if there's anything else you can do to make their time with you more productive and enjoyable.

Prepare registration personnel adequately.

With those that will be handling the registration, be certain to go over the script you'd like them to be reciting. Even write it down. It might go something like: "Hi, welcome to San Diego Ad Expo. May I confirm your last name? ... Inside your package, you will find... Your first session will be held down the hall and ..."

Set up special arrangements for speakers.

You will likely designate a special line for your speakers. If at all possible, use your program chair as personnel here. He or she will be acquainted with the speakers and will be a familiar name to welcome them.

Don't take on unnecessary responsibilities.

It's also important to communicate to staff exactly what its jurisdiction should be. Let them know what questions you want them to answer and which you want directed elsewhere.

For example, you probably don't want your staff to be responsible for giving out advice about where to go for dinner or which neighborhoods are safe to walk in. This is an area better handled by the concierge or doorman. Even if a staff member had a wonderful experience at a restaurant in China Town last year, it doesn't mean something hasn't changed since then. Should one of your attendees contract food poisoning at a restaurant your staff had suggested, your organization could be held liable. At the very least, you could have a potential public image disaster on your hands. Instead, give this responsibility to those better informed, to those that make it their job to know the very latest about the city—the latest safety concerns, the most highly acclaimed nearby attractions and the most current restaurant reviews.

If you're planning a large meeting and have the budget, consider hiring the hotel's concierge or a member of the chamber of commerce to person a booth at your registration to answer attendees' questions about taking in the city. Otherwise, simply instruct your people to defer these questions to the hotel staff, who obviously will have better and more up-to-date information.

CONSIDER A "SOFT" REGISTRATION OPENING

A dress rehearsal would be an ideal way to spot errors in your system or delinquencies in your training. Unfortunately, there's no realistic way to do this. However, here's an idea. Open your registration one or two hours earlier than the published time. There will be a few folks that will meander down to registration early. Now, before the rush happens, watch to see if there's anything you missed in the training and take the opportunity to reinforce those issues. This way, when the flood gates open, everyone will be totally prepared and you, as a meeting planner, can feel confident that everyone knows what you want them to do.

USE YOUR STAFF WISELY

Design systems that best accommodate your rush times. For example, say you're managing registration of a trade show. If the trade show starts at 11:00 - even if registration starts at 9:00 - when is everyone going to show up? About eight minutes to 11:00. So you're going to have three hundred people in line wanting to get through as quickly as possible. If your trade show lasts three hours and you take an hour and a half to get everyone processed, that's not going to make your exhibitors very happy. They want the people on the floor.

So, design a process that anticipates typical attendee behavior, one that allows you to capture the information, issue the badge and ID number and get them inside the show. After the big influx, keep your staff on for a couple more hours to bring the files back out and enter the data while it's slow.

IN THE EVENT OF AN EMERGENCY

Make sure the staff has the information and the processes in order to handle emergencies. If someone's family calls your meeting needing to get in touch with one of your attendees, will you be able to handle the situation? Do you know where each of your attendees is staying?

FEED 'EM IF YOU NEED 'EM

If you want to keep your customers happy, it's important to keep your employees happy. One easy way to do this is to keep them fed during on-site office hours. You can work with the hotel catering to create a lunch in your staff office. Or you can order off the room service menu. You might create a relatively inexpensive buffet of club or sub sandwiches and have them cut in half. Hardly anyone will eat a full sandwich. Couple these with some small salads, chips, sodas and water and you've got hearty sustenance for your crew. By the way, this will probably be less taxing on your budget than giving everyone an expense account or per diem.

IT'S ALMOST CURTAIN CALL

Now, you've arrived at the property and have checked to ensure that all your supplies have also arrived safely. You've got about 36 hours before show time. How are you going to make sure everything comes together without a hitch?

Probably the first thing you'll want to do once you've directed your staff to start setting up the office is to meet with the hotel contact and once again walk through the space. Make sure that all your meeting's pertinent information will be displayed on the hotel's placards and in-house television.

Then walk through the hotel and determine where your directional signage will have to go. You want to make it as easy as possible for any attendee to find you, so place signs and arrows from any possible direction someone could approach your registration table.

CURTAIN'S UP: YOU'RE ON-SITE!

You've been working very hard for the last several months to make this meeting a success. While you're in the home stretch, there's still a bit more work to do.

BE READY TO MAKE THE BEST IMPRESSION POSSIBLE

Think through the registration process and make sure that you've considered everything while you still can make arrangements.

DON'T FORGET GEORGE

As we mentioned, your typical attendee, whom we're calling George, has had a horrible last day and a half. After rushing around like a banshee to get out of town, he's had to hurry up and wait for every airline connection, shuttle service and for his room to finally be ready.

Remember, your attendee, more often than not, will show up at your registration counter having had a similar experience to George's. And it's likely that you'll be the one to blame. "Why did you send this brochure to me? It's all your fault I had such an awful day. I don't want to be here. Why did I sign up for this?"

Your registration, as the first impression your attendees have of your meeting, is your chance to reinforce the positive aspects of making the decision to be there. So, you want it to run as seamlessly as possible.

MAKE YOUR REGISTRATION COUNTER FEEL LIKE HOME

Your registration counter doesn't have to look sterile and corporate. With a couple of simple touches, you can create a warm and inviting welcome. Add a couple of plants, a few vases of flowers and some warm, incandescent lamps and you've got a totally different feel.

One meeting planner collects all the inexpensive vases he and his wife receive, ships them to the meeting and fills them with a few stems of the prettiest flowers he can find at a nearby grocery store. He also makes arrangements with the hotel to place a few of the house plants in the registration area and room lamps along the registration counter. It creates a welcoming, homey feel.

You want your registration counter to exude the attitude you want. Be creative. If you're managing a meeting for an edgy cosmetology company, you might want to add some techno touches. If it's for a group of sports agents, you might consider … well, you get the idea.

LET THEM EAT CANDY

Here's another attitude adjustment trick.

Put out several bowls of candy for your patrons to enjoy.

Have you every tried being mad with a piece of candy in your mouth? Candy immediately gets your weary travelers' sugar levels up. More often than not, their attitudes will change immediately.

PREPARE FOR EFFICIENCY

Doesn't it always seem that the more you're in a hurry, the more time the group in front of you takes? Waiting in line is no fun for anyone. You will want to set up your registration lines to be the most efficient possible.

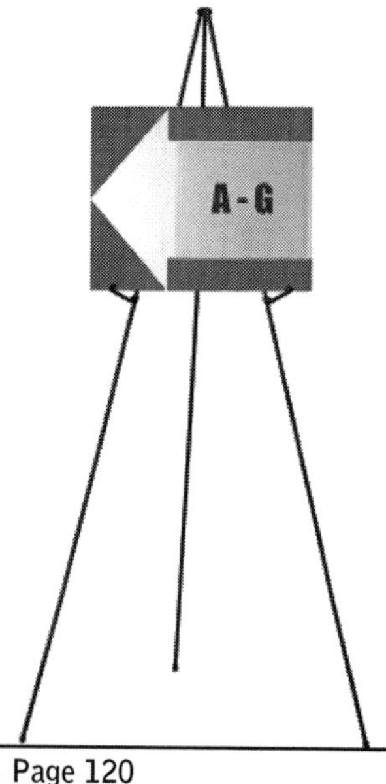

There are several ways to set up an efficient registration. If you are expecting a lot of on-site registrations, you might want to snake your lines as they do at the airport. This allows attendees to go to the first available counter and keeps the line moving.

On the other hand, if most of your attendees are pre-registered, you might want to break out separate lines for your various attendees.

The most typical split is alphabetized pre-registrants, speakers, VIPs and on-site

MEETING REGISTRATION A-L M-Z

registrants.

To separate your pre-registrant lines into the most efficient groups, go through your list and find the most logical divisions.

It doesn't always make sense to just divide the alphabet in half or thirds.

Look at your own list. Perhaps if it's a convention for Irish descendants, you'll need a line for just M-O's (McCoys and O'Connors) Or you might need a single line just for the S's. Once you've determined how to best divide your group, you'll need to order the proper signage to arrive on site when you need it.

REMEMBER SECURITY

While you want to make your registration to appear as inviting as possible, you also want the back of the house to be as professional, secure and buttoned-down as possible.

Think about it. A table selling T-shirts and books can easily have $3,000 to $4,000 in cash on hand at any given time. Moreover, a meeting that's accepting on-site registrations could take in over $20,000 within a couple of hours. Cash-on-hand is a magnet for trouble makers. Meetings are an especially "easy target" as they are not set up to handle cash day in and day out.

Or so one might think...

Make sure you take all the possible precautions to keep your meeting and your attendees as secure as possible.

PLAY IT SAFE

Prearrange to have access to the hotel vault each night. In addition to locking up all your cash and checks, also use the vault to store any credit card carbons or slips. Never leave them in the trash or in the hotel room. They all should go into the vault for the protection of your meeting and of your attendees. It's also a good idea to arrange for a room safe at the registration or sales table. While you should never leave money or valuables in this safe when the counter is unattended or over night, it's a good way to keep things secure during the hustle of a busy registration. It's also a good place to keep purses or keys so they aren't readily accessible.

CONSIDER HIRING SECURITY

You might want to consider a security guard (undercover or uniformed) at your registration counter if you anticipate taking in large sums of money. The mere presence of a uniformed guard might dissuade any dishonest behavior.

REVIEW YOUR INSURANCE COVERAGE

You might not realize the amount of exposure you're opening yourself up to while you're on site and away from the office. Review your policy with your agent. Make sure that you are insured for at least the amount of cash you're going to be taking in. As you're not likely covered to take in that much cash every day, you might need to take out a rider to cover the occasional meeting. However, if you do many meetings a year, it might be less expensive to raise your limits rather than adding a temporary rider for each meeting you manage.

For: Sharon ☐ URGENT
Date: 7/6 Time: 10:30 am

WHILE YOU WERE OUT

M Angie Brown
Of:
Phone: area code number extension

☐ Called ☐ Please call
☒ Stoped by ☐ Will call back
☐ Returned your call ☐ Wants to see you

Message: Sharon, I'm in room 702. Call me when you get in
Angie

Signed:

MANAGE MESSAGE BOARDS

Many meetings arrange to have message boards near the registration area so attendees can communicate with each other. This is an extremely easy way to help facilitate networking and deter your busy staff from having to be message takers. However, use precautions. Always fold the message over so only the name line shows. Otherwise your attendees might be broadcasting risky information to anyone who passes by. If an attendee wants to let her friend know that she's in town and checked in she might write something like: "Sharon, Call me when you get in. I'm in room 702, Angie Brown." That's all the information someone would need to be able to order the most expensive lobster dinner in the hotel restaurant and charge it to the unsuspecting Ms. Brown.

KEEP CONTROL OF BADGE STOCK

Remember, at most meetings, badge stock is as good as money. So, keep it well protected.

It's not that difficult for an attendee to grab a blank meeting badge and have it imprinted with a friend's name for entry into the $100/plate banquet or the Universal Studios® Tour. So, keep your extra stock under lock and key and instruct your staff to be very careful with it. Also, make sure that staff knows to rip up and throw away any misprints that have to be replaced. An imposter would not care if Tony Shell's name is misspelled and could easily grab it from the garbage to use it to get into your meeting.

In addition to your own financial risk, misplaced badges can pose a corporate espionage threat to your sponsoring organization. All it would take for an employee of Cola Giant A to sneak into Cola Giant B's announcement of next year's sales strategy would be an extra name badge carelessly left in the waste basket.

Also create a process for replacing lost cards. You're likely to have at least a couple attendees who forgot their pre-mailed badge at home or left their badge at a restaurant. Most of the time, these claims will be legitimate. However, to dissuade the one who's trying to get an extra badge to get his buddy into the party, you might consider having everyone requesting a new badge sign a waiver that spells out that prosecution will occur if anything fraudulent is suspected.

OFFER A SAFETY REMINDER

During your housekeeping announcements give a short safety presentation just to remind infrequent travelers what they can do to keep themselves safe. You might make suggestions such as:

- Always double-bolt the hotel door.
- Leave the TV on while you're out of the room.
- Look through the peep hole before answering the door.
- Use the room safe if you bring along valuables.
- If you're leaving the hotel alone, let someone know where you're going and when you'll be back.
- Avoid walking in strange neighborhoods.
- Take taxi cabs.
- Don't wear your badge out of the hotel. Doing so screams out to potential attackers "Hey, I don't belong here and I likely have a bunch of cash on me."

BACK UP EARLY AND OFTEN

Create systems and provide provisions to back up your data and to have back up computers at your disposal. Remember, your data is one of your most valuable assets. All you need is a power surge, a dead battery or a crashed computer to find yourself in a whole lot of trouble.

First, you should have a Plan B in the event you arrive on-site and find your computer doesn't work. You might prepare one of your laptop computers as a backup or, at least, have investigated a resource for renting a compatible computer. It is unlikely that you will have the occasion to have to resort to Plan B, but you will be very glad should you ever need it.

Next, provide your staff with the procedures and provisions to back up your data periodically. Depending on the size of your database and your computers capabilities, you could back up to a disk or CD. Another alternative is to purchase an external drive, such as a thumb drive. This nifty gadget, which is no bigger than a pack of gum, plugs into a basic USB port and can store several gigs of information.

Should you rent a computer, be sure to wipe off the hard drive before you return it so you don't unwittingly send your attendees' personal credit card information to the rental house, or worse to the next renter. It's your responsibility to ensure that there is no data left on any machine that you return.

HOTEL AND MOTEL FIRE SAFETY

From the National Fire Protection Agency

BEFORE A FIRE

- When making a hotel reservation or checking into a hotel, ask about the fire safety features of the facility and choose a facility that's protected by both smoke alarms and is fully fire sprinklered.
- When checking in, ask what the fire alarm system sound is for the facility.
- Become familiar with the fire escape plan posted in your room.
- Locate the two nearest stairs and count the number of doors between your room and the stairwell. In a fire, the hall may be dark and it may be difficult to see the exit stairway. Counting the number of doors may help you find the stairs.
- Look for exit signs wherever you are in the facility.
- Check to make sure the exits are not locked or blocked. Notify the hotel manager if exits are not accessible.
- Keep your room key by your nightstand so that you can easily reach it in an emergency.
- Travel with a flashlight and fresh batteries in case the power goes out.
- Report any unusual behavior or fire hazards to hotel management.

DURING A FIRE

- If the fire alarm sounds, leave the building immediately. Take your room key with you, in case the exits are blocked by fire or smoke, you can return to your room.
- Test doors before you open them. If there is fire on the other side, it will feel warm around the cracks. If the door is warm, use your second way out or stay in your room and begin procedures for "If You Are Trapped." If the door is cool, open it cautiously and check to make sure your escape path is clear of fire and smoke.
- Always use the stairs, not an elevator, during a fire.
- If you must escape through smoke, crawl low under the smoke on your hands and knees to your exit.

IF YOU ARE TRAPPED

- If you can't escape and there's not fire in your room, stay put.
- Call the fire department and let them know your exact location.
- Shut off fans and air conditioners because they can draw smoke into the room.
- Stuff towels or sheets in the cracks around all doors and vents between you and the fire.
- If you can, open the window at the top and bottom, but be prepared to shut it if smoke comes into the room. Do not break the window so that you are able to shut it if needed.
- Stay at the window and signal the firefighters by waving a light-colored cloth or a flash light.

FOLLOW THROUGH- DON'T FORGET TO EVALUATE

Evaluation is one of the most important aspects of the successful meeting planner's job. An effective evaluation process not only demonstrates how well you've been able to meet your goals, but also allows you to discover ways to improve future meetings. Evaluations can also be an excellent communication tool to demonstrate to bosses, clients or prospective customers how you were able to deliver on each of their objectives.

BENEFITS OF EVALUATION:

- Detect your meetings' weaknesses
- Suggest areas needing improvement
- Discover ways to make your program better
- Determine your intangible return on investment
- Learn more about your audiences' needs and desires
- Gather testimonials for next year's meeting marketing
- Collect information for hotel audit

WHAT SHOULD YOU EVALUATE?

It's important to evaluate every aspect of your meeting or conference—from the registration process, to the on-site experience, to the value of each of the educational sessions. You'll also want to query your speakers, sponsors and exhibitors to better understand how they experienced your processes and level of service.

If you don't evaluate each aspect of the meeting, you may come away with a skewed vision of the success, or failings, of your overall performance.

YOU'LL LIKELY TO WANT TO EVALUATE:

REGISTRATION

- Pre-registration process
- Registration form

- Price
- Ease of registration
- On-site registration
- Customer service
- How an attendee heard about you
- Suggestions for improvements in the future

MEETING SITE

- Location city
- Meeting facility
- Hotel accommodations
- Food
- Customer service

PROGRAM

- Topics
- Speaker quality
- Educational atmosphere
- Audio visual
- Staffing
- Suggestions for future topics or speakers

SPECIAL ACTIVITIES

- Receptions/Banquets/Luncheons
- Tours
- Local attractions

TRADE SHOW

- Quality and number of exhibitors
- Layout and presentation

ATTENDEE PROFILE

To better plan and market next year's conference, you'll want to gather demographic data on this year's attendees and exhibitors.

EVALUATION DESIGN

Keep it simple. You want to design your evaluation to solicit clear and meaningful information. Usually a combination of closed-ended ratings and open-ended questions will give you the best overall impression of your event. Rating strategies allow you to numerically quantify and compare various aspects of your conference, as well as your success from year to year. Open-ended questions may give you a better idea of why the attendee chose a specific rating and can give you excellent suggestions for future years.

EVALUATION COLLECTION

There are many ways to collect evaluation feedback. You can either use traditional, paper evaluations on site or you can direct attendees to go home and submit their feedback via the Internet.

If you go the traditional route, you might want to consider evaluating program sessions immediately after participation and then of the overall conference experience at the very end of the event.

For the budget that allows for room monitors, this is an excellent way to gather evaluations on individual workshops or events. Essentially, the attendee has to hand in the filled out evaluation to be able to leave the room.

Drop Evaluations Here

Large, bright, clearly-labeled boxes can also be strategically placed outside the session door or at the back of the room to collect immediate feed back.

Many meeting planners include an overall evaluation of the meeting in the registration package and scatter collection boxes all around the meeting space for attendees to drop in their evaluations at their own convenience.

Some meeting planners choose to collect this information over the Internet using a survey tool on their own website or by an independent survey service, such as Zoomerang™.

These types of services provide the added benefit of accurate evaluation design and timely, thorough analysis. This can take a lot of burden off of the meeting planner who does not feel comfortable with his or her training in this area or doesn't have the time to devote to this essential task.

For more information about one example of this type of service, see http://info.zoomerang.com.

TIMING IS EVERYTHING

One of the most important aspects of creating a meaningful evaluation process is to commit to the immediate collection, analysis and summation of the feedback. Often times, the busy meeting planner is already thinking about the next meeting during the final hours of this one.

If the data is not immediately processed, it is very easy to allow it to land in the "TO DO" basket, where it soon makes its way to the bottom of the heap. Then, it becomes a nagging burden that grows to a seemingly Goliath task.

When, and if, the meeting planner finally gets back to it, the feedback may be less meaningful because the details and immediacy of the meeting have long since been blurred by more recent meetings and obligations.

Early in the planning stages of your meeting, it is a good idea to specifically designate the personnel and deadlines for evaluating data analysis while still on site or immediately upon returning to the office.

INSPIRE ATTENDEE PARTICIPATION

After you've carefully designed your evaluation and committed resources to its prompt compilation and analysis, you'll want to do all that you can to inspire all attendees to return their filled out evaluations.

Meeting planners have several tools and tricks for collecting evaluations.

Some meeting planners have designed inspirational tricks to help ensure they receive as many returned evaluations as possible. For example, one meeting planner sets up a table at the end of the meeting or individual workshop. The attendees only get their copies of the meeting notes and materials when they hand in their evaluations.

Another meeting planner brings a printer on site and creates customized certificates acknowledging individuals' participation. Of course, attendees can only receive their certificates upon completion of their evaluation.

This is a chance for the meeting planner to be creative. You might consider holding a drawing or giving away door prizes or handing out meeting-branded specialty items as a reward for participation.

GOIN' AROUND THE BLOCK

One of the biggest problems for a meeting planner is hotel attrition. A common requirement these days is for a hotel to receive 80-85% of the reserved block to avoid having to pay for all the unused rooms in that block. This makes running a profitable meeting more difficult than ever. There is a lot of pressure on the meeting planner to get an early and accurate count so that he or she can comfortably guarantee the proper size of room block needed.

The advent of the Internet has complicated this problem. Today, it is pretty easy for an attendee to search the destination city for cheaper accommodations. Without adequate inspiration to book at the host hotel, many meeting planners are finding their attendees are making their own hotel arrangements at other nearby properties.

This can be extremely frustrating for the meeting planner. However, even more frustrating is when attendees "go around the block."

This is a relatively new phenomenon. Here's how it works. The attendees get online and search websites such as hotel.com, priceline.com, travelocity.com or orbitz.com to find better prices for the host hotel. Then, they book it themselves. Meeting planners who aren't on top of the game, won't get credit for those hotel rooms they faithfully marketed through their materials, but that weren't booked through them.

To properly get credit for one's hard work and marketing investment, savvy meeting planners use the evaluation process to audit actual host hotel use. Meeting planners that ask the question on the evaluation, "where did you stay?," might have the ammunition to go back to the property to prove that they actually did meet the hotel block requirements. The courts have been ruling that rooms purchased at the convention hotel through these other sources need to be credited to the meeting planner's necessary quota.

So, it's become extremely important to ask on the evaluation form, "where are you staying?" and have the attendees sign their evaluation forms as evidence that the hotel block was successfully filled.

Ways to inspire attendees to register through the meeting planner:

- Require a higher registration fee for those that make their own accommodation plans
- Offer a lower registration fee for those that do make all arrangements through you
- Restrict access to special attendee privileges such as use of the cyber café or free exhibition rights

IT'S ALL ABOUT THE FOLLOW THROUGH

Remember that evaluation is a very important aspect of a meeting planner's success. At the end of a conference, after months or years of planning and preparation, just when you're likely to want to do nothing more than fall onto the couch or rush into the next project, it's critical to finish the project with a timely and thorough evaluation of your meeting.

Be a Tiger.

As you know, the world-famous golf champion would never have become a household word if he allowed his swing to break just short of the perfect and complete follow through.

Good luck.

Get out there. Keep your eye on the ball...
....and don't forget to have a whole lot of fun!

SAMPLE OVERALL EVALUATION

REGISTRATION

Please rate the following:	Excellent	Very Good	Fair	Poor	Not Applicable
Quality of conference announcement	❑	❑	❑	❑	❑
Quality of conference update communication	❑	❑	❑	❑	❑
Frequency of conference update communication	❑	❑	❑	❑	❑
Website conference information	❑	❑	❑	❑	❑
Quality of email communications	❑	❑	❑	❑	❑
Frequency of email communications	❑	❑	❑	❑	❑
Registration form	❑	❑	❑	❑	❑
Overall ease of registration	❑	❑	❑	❑	❑
Quality of hotel reservation customer service	❑	❑	❑	❑	❑
"Early Bird" registration price	❑	❑	❑	❑	❑
Conference Price	❑	❑	❑	❑	❑
Overall cost to attend	❑	❑	❑	❑	❑
On-site registration experience	❑	❑	❑	❑	❑
On-site member services (Cyber Café, etc.)	❑	❑	❑	❑	❑
Conference customer service	❑	❑	❑	❑	❑
Registration package	❑	❑	❑	❑	❑

How did you first hear of this conference? ______________________________

Your suggestions for improving communication ______________________________

and registration? ______________________________

MEETING SITE

	Excellent	Very Good	Fair	Poor	Not Applicable
Desirability of location city	❑	❑	❑	❑	❑
Meeting facility	❑	❑	❑	❑	❑
Value and quality of hotel accommodations	❑	❑	❑	❑	❑
Hotel check-in/check-out	❑	❑	❑	❑	❑
Overall hotel experience	❑	❑	❑	❑	❑
Hotel food and beverage offerings	❑	❑	❑	❑	❑
Conference transportation	❑	❑	❑	❑	❑
Conference customer service	❑	❑	❑	❑	❑

Name of hotel in which you stayed: ______________________________

Your suggestions for improvements in the future? ______________________________

SAMPLE OVERALL EVALUATION #2

PROGRAM	Excellent	Very Good	Fair	Poor	Not Applicable
Selection of education topics	❑	❑	❑	❑	❑
Number of sessions offered	❑	❑	❑	❑	❑
Satisfaction of educational objectives	❑	❑	❑	❑	❑
Satisfaction of networking objectives	❑	❑	❑	❑	❑
Speaker quality	❑	❑	❑	❑	❑
Educational atmosphere	❑	❑	❑	❑	❑
Quality of audio visual support	❑	❑	❑	❑	❑
Availability and helpfulness of meeting staff	❑	❑	❑	❑	❑

Suggestions for improvements, future topics or speakers ______________________________

____

____

SPECIAL ACTIVITIES	Excellent	Very Good	Fair	Poor	Not Applicable
Opening reception	❑	❑	❑	❑	❑
Continental breakfasts and breaks	❑	❑	❑	❑	❑
Banquets	❑	❑	❑	❑	❑
Luncheons	❑	❑	❑	❑	❑
Tours	❑	❑	❑	❑	❑
Golf outing	❑	❑	❑	❑	❑
Local attractions	❑	❑	❑	❑	❑

Your suggestions for improvements in the future? ______________________________

____

____

TRADE SHOW	Excellent	Very Good	Fair	Poor	Not Applicable
Quality and number of exhibitors	❑	❑	❑	❑	❑
Relevance of exhibitors to your profession	❑	❑	❑	❑	❑
Layout and presentation	❑	❑	❑	❑	❑

Your suggestions for improvements in the future? ______________________________

____

____

SAMPLE ATTENDEE PROFILE & MEETING EXPERIENCE QUESTIONS

To better plan and market next year's conference, you'll want to gather demographic data on your attendees and exhibitors this year. Use this tool to customize questions to meet your own meeting information needs as well as to the specific audience you're speaking to.

HELP US DO A BETTER JOB OF SERVING YOU...

In an effort to better design future events, please take a moment and tell us a little more about you and your professional needs.

Please let us know which best describes you....

Age	17-22	23-30	31-35	36-41	42-55	56-64	65+
Gender	Male	Female					
Years in the industry	under 2	2-5	6-10	11-20	over 20		
Years as a member	under 2	2-5	6-10	11-20	over 20	❑ not a member	
Average number of conferences you attend each year	0-1	2-3	4-5	6-7	8-9	more than 10	

What was your main reason for attending this meeting?

❑ Education ❑ Networking ❑ Business Generation ❑ Support of industry ❑ Other_______________

Who paid for your registration fee?

❑ Employer ❑ Self ❑ Complimentary ❑ Other _______________

Do you plan to attend this meeting next year?

❑ Yes ❑ No ❑ Undecided Why or why not?_______________

Which best describes the organization for which you work?

❑ Corporation ❑ Government ❑ University ❑ Non-profit ❑ Association ❑ Retail

Which best describes your role in your organization?

❑ President/Owner ❑ Senior Manager ❑ Middle Manager ❑ Entry Level ❑ AE/Sales ❑ Other_________

Do you authorize expenditures for equipment or services?

❑ Yes ❑ No (If no, you can skip the next two questions)

Approximately, how much do you spend annually with the following?
(Add list of products and services relevant to the industry and the exhibitors of your meeting)

Approximately, how much do you spend annually on business expenses?
Professional Development: $__________ Legal: $__________ Accounting: $________Consulting: $__________
Shipping: $__________ Office Supplies: $__________Insurance: $__________
DSL/Cable/Internet Access: $__________ Telephone: $__________ Other:_______________ $__________

What suggestions do you have to improve this event next year?
____
____
____

SAMPLE EDUCATION PROGRAM EVALUATION

TITLE OF SESSION________________________ **DATE**__________________

PRESENTER'S NAME____________________________________

SPEAKER

Please rate the following:	Excellent	Very Good	Fair	Poor	Not Applicable
Command of subject knowledge	❑	❑	❑	❑	❑
Quality of delivery style	❑	❑	❑	❑	❑
Amount of interaction with the audience	❑	❑	❑	❑	❑
Degree to which the speaker held my attention	❑	❑	❑	❑	❑
Quality of audio-visual support	❑	❑	❑	❑	❑
Quality of handout materials	❑	❑	❑	❑	❑
Amount of new information learned	❑	❑	❑	❑	❑
Worthiness of bringing back this speaker	❑	❑	❑	❑	❑

Comments ____________________________________

____

____

SUBJECT MATTER

Please rate the following:	Excellent	Very Good	Fair	Poor	Not Applicable
Amount of relevance this subject has to my profession	❑	❑	❑	❑	❑
Degree to which this subject is of interest to me	❑	❑	❑	❑	❑
Degree to which you will be able to use this information	❑	❑	❑	❑	❑
Worthiness of repeating this topic	❑	❑	❑	❑	❑

Comments ____________________________________

____

Were your professional goals and objectives met during this session? ________________

____

____

What did you learn that you'll be able to use once you return to the office? ________________

____

____

What didn't you learn that you thought you would? ________________

____

____

SAMPLE EXHIBITOR EVALUATION

Please share your comments on having been an exhibitor with us. Your feedback will be used to plan and improve future conferences.

EXHIBITOR EXPERIENCE

Please rate the following:	Excellent	Very Good	Fair	Poor	Not Applicable
Pre-conference information and materials	❑	❑	❑	❑	❑
Registration process	❑	❑	❑	❑	❑
Quality of customer service provided to you	❑	❑	❑	❑	❑
before the event	❑	❑	❑	❑	❑
Level of service rendered to you during the event	❑	❑	❑	❑	❑
Quality of overall facility	❑	❑	❑	❑	❑
Amount of time allowed for set up and strike	❑	❑	❑	❑	❑
Ability to network with attendees	❑	❑	❑	❑	❑
Cost of booth	❑	❑	❑	❑	❑
Additional activities	❑	❑	❑	❑	❑

Comments ______________________________

____

____

EXHIBITOR SERVICES COMPANY

Please rate the following:	Excellent	Very Good	Fair	Poor	Not Applicable
Level of service	❑	❑	❑	❑	❑
Pricing	❑	❑	❑	❑	❑
Variety of products made available to you	❑	❑	❑	❑	❑

Comments ______________________________

____

____

Were your business objectives met during this conference? ______________________________

____

How did you hear about this conference?

❑ Referral ❑ Direct mail ❑ Website ❑ Association news ❑ Other______________________________

Will you return next year as an exhibitor?

❑ Yes ❑ No ❑ Undecided Why or why not?______________________________

Include your name and affiliation (optional)

____

____

INDEX